The
RESCUE
DOG
BUCKET
LIST

Alexandra T. Kleinkopf

ACKNOWLEDGEMENTS

A special thank you to dog aficionado Dawn Alvarado for her excellent suggestions on safety, training, keeping it humane, and much more.

Thank you also to those who contributed personal stories about adoption and foster experiences. It was such a joy to hear them firsthand and to see all of your heartwarming photos.

And finally, to Ryan, for his unlimited support, and for patiently waiting for me to go out and play with him while I was busy writing.

13-Digit ISBN: 9781604336078
10-Digit ISBN: 1604336072

This book may be ordered by mail from the publisher. Please include $4.95 for postage and handling. Please support your local bookseller first!

Books published by Cider Mill Press Book Publishers are available at special discounts for bulk purchases in the United States by corporations, institutions, and other organizations. For more information, please contact the publisher.

Cider Mill Press Book Publishers
"Where good books are ready for press"
PO Box 454
12 Spring Street
Kennebunkport, Maine 04046

Visit us on the Web! www.cidermillpress.com

Cover design by Shelby Newsted
Interior design by Mark Voss Design

Photo Credits:
Personal Photographs in the "Real-Life Adoption Stories" Chapter are provided courtesy of the wonderful dog owners featured.
Brad & Scarlet photos are courtesy of Bradford Perry
Jacqueline & Blake photos are courtesy of Jacqueline Yorke
Dane & Honey photos are courtesy of Dane Berry
Casey, Staci & Spottie photos are courtesy of Casey & Staci Childs
Chris & Chata photos are courtesy of Christopher Regis
Katie & Keeper photos are courtesy of Katie VanTassell
Ashley & Coco and Jayson & Bucky photos are courtesy of Ashley Greene
Lori & Lilly photos are courtesy of Lori Lee Polk
Mardu, Ron & their Troop photos are courtesy of Mardu Lydick
Max & Morrison photos are courtesy of Max Weiner
Ray & Casey photos are courtesy of Raymond Thomas
Simone & Taj photos are courtesy of Simone Stemper; the photograph featuring the leash in snow is credited to Benoy Varghese
All other images are used under official license from Shutterstock.com

Printed in China

1 2 3 4 5 6 7 8 9 0
First Edition

The RESCUE DOG BUCKET LIST

Alexandra T. Kleinkopf

CONTENTS

Foreword P.8

Introduction P.10

Getting to Know You P.12

A Dog Behavior Primer for the Two-Legged P.38

The Rescue Dog's Bag of Tricks P.54

Happily Ever After: Real-Life Adoption Stories P.95

- Brad & Scarlet
- Jacqueline & Blake
- Dane & Honey
- Casey, Staci & Spottie
- Chris & Chata
- Katie & Keeper
- Ashley & Coco and Jayson & Bucky
- Lori & Lilly
- Mardu, Ron & their Troop
- Max & Morrison
- Ray & Casey
- Simone & Taj

Resources P.154

FOREWORD

I have felt an undeniable, special connection to animals since I was a small child and have had the joy of pets in my home throughout my entire adult life—never being without the unconditional love and companionship of a dog. These lovable creatures are a source of friendship, support, and even entertainment through the best and worst of times. They are my confidants, hobby partners, and exercise buddies. They love me no matter what—all-forgiving and all-accepting. They are truly a gift like no other—which is why I committed my life to making sure that all homeless pets find a loving home and that no one is denied the joy I have found in being the proud parent of a rescued dog. There are still thousands and thousands of great dogs awaiting their second chapter and I believe it is our responsibility to give them the life they deserve.

DIANE BLANKENBURG, CEO OF THE HUMANE NETWORK

"A dog is the only
thing on earth
that loves you more
than he loves himself."

JOSH BILLINGS

INTRODUCTION

It's the rare person who will walk into a car dealership and select a pre-owned vehicle with as much enthusiasm as if he were given the chance to take home the same exact model, brand new. No new car smell and no blank slate to start from, just a collection of slightly worn parts, undiscovered idiosyncrasies, and sometimes even problems that once frustrated somebody else.

The person who walks into an animal rescue or shelter is faced with a similar situation—these animals are not blank slates. They do not come with extended warranties, and there is seldom a disclosure form or documentation of past accidents or incidents.

They are the take-me-as-I-am option, the collection of slightly worn parts, undiscovered idiosyncrasies, and sometimes even problems that once frustrated somebody else. But dogs are not cars, and chances are you are not the kind of dog person who shies away from a "pre-owned" animal to make a beeline for the newest model in the pet store window. You are an adopter, a fosterer, a nurturer—a savior to the animal you've taken home.

The truth is, your journey with your rescue dog will probably not be without its bumps. The first day euphoria will gently dissipate, and the realities of being a primary caregiver will come into focus. There will be inconveniences, there will be worry, and yes, there will be bills! There may also be breakdowns and perhaps even the sinking fear that you've made a mistake.

However, this road you are on together is like none other you can imagine—unless, of course, you have rescued a dog before. It is a journey of trust, mutual support, unconditional love, and intermittent comedy that revives the soul and results in a strong, meaningful bond. It is the kind of road that makes you forget where you're going, because the ride itself has been such a worthwhile experience.

In this text, I hope you will find inspiration, helpful information, and perhaps even the etchings of a road map, if this is your first time on this journey. By no means is this book intended to circumscribe all there is to know about dogs or adoption, but rather to serve as a jumping off point to get you headed in the right direction.

The Resources section at the back is also a useful, albeit incomplete, compass to guide you as you get started. Adopting a dog is a true commitment and also a promise to someone you've only just met—a living creature whose personal development will be directly and noticeably impacted by you, the person at the center of their universe. Through whatever challenges you may face together down the road, your importance to this animal will remain paramount. For all the rescued dogs and those still waiting to be welcomed into nurturing homes, I commend you, the adopter, for taking the road less traveled.

GETTING TO KNOW YOU
TIPS FOR ACCLIMATING YOUR DOG—AND YOURSELF—TO A NEW HOUSEHOLD.

Congratulations on taking the plunge! Now that you've officially decided to foster or adopt a dog, you're about to discover just how rich and rewarding your life together can be. But as is the case with any new parents, your next-day arrival may naturally feel a little overwhelming at first. Below are some suggestions and guidance to help you through that preliminary period of "Oh my God … I've got a dog!"

FIRST THINGS FIRST

Bringing home a new dog can sort of be like bringing home a new baby. It involves a lot of adjustment on everyone's part, and the more you prepare for the arrival ahead of time, the better your chances are of having a smooth transition. Make sure you have all the necessary supplies in order before you bring your rescue home. That includes a leash, a collar, food and water dishes, a crate, bedding … you name it.

Run through a plan in your head of how the homecoming and first couple of days will go. Walk through each hour of the day, step by step, to help illuminate anything you may have forgotten that still needs attention, such as dog-proofing your living room. Also decide what the house rules will be for your dog, in order to reduce confusion and conflicting signals during what is bound to already be a slightly confusing time for both of you.

Before bringing your dog home from the shelter or rescue, have an ID tag made up with his or her name and your contact information. That way, if Lady wanders off, she won't wind up in a shelter again awaiting adoption! Eventually, having your vet mircochip your dog is one of the most effective ways to ensure she's returned to you if she ever gets lost. Remember to register the chip and update your contact info if you move or change phone numbers.

"Outside of a dog, a book is man's best friend. Inside of a dog it's too dark to read."

GROUCHO MARX

BUCKET LIST

5 FOODIE ACTIVITIES

For any pup who fully embraces the joy of eating,
these five ideas are food for thought.
Turn the page to read more about each one!

- ☐ COOK A DOG-FRIENDLY MEAL FROM SCRATCH
- ☐ PICK UP A DOG-FRIENDLY BRAND OF ICE CREAM FOR DESSERT
- ☐ DINE AT A CANINE-FRIENDLY RESTAURANT
- ☐ HAVE A BACKYARD BARBEQUE AND INVITE OTHER FURRY FRIENDS
- ☐ BAKE MUFFINS WITH DOG-SAFE INGREDIENTS

FIVE ACTIVITIES FOR CANINE FOODIES

Meal Appeal

For a change of pace from kibble, try cooking a dog-friendly meal for your four-legged pal that you can enjoy together. Unseasoned ingredients like boneless boiled chicken and cooked plain rice can be a healthy alternative and add some welcome variety once in a while, if your vet gives the OK.

Melting Hearts and Desserts

Next time you take a trip for your favorite frozen confection—even if it's just to the freezer—pick up a dog-friendly brand of ice cream for Scout to savor. Or, if you're a DIYer and your vet gives her blessing, whip up your own recipe with all-natural ingredients like yogurt, coconut milk, peanut butter, honey and fruit. Same rules apply for dogs as for kids: dessert after dinner, and only in moderation!

Growling Tummies? Grab a Bite

More and more restaurants are permitting dogs to accompany diners, so whether you're planning a meal out, or you decide to sit down for an impromptu snack with a furry companion of a less discerning palate, you needn't retreat back home for leftovers.

Grills, Burgers and Dogs

Fire up the grill, crack open some cold ones, and bust out a game of Cornhole, horseshoes, Frisbee, croquet, Badminton … whatever your tradition is. Encourage friends and family to bring their pups, so everyone gets a chance to socialize, play, and stuff their faces. Hold the onions, chicken bones, and chocolate desserts for the pups though; they're off-limits for dogs.

He Loves your Muffin Top(s)

If you love to bake, or just want to try your hand at it, baking muffins with dog-friendly ingredients is an easy and delicious way to share a moment with a good boy or girl who seldom gets to try any of those delicious things that come out of the oven.

Your dog will experience a lot of overnight changes when you bring her home, but diet should probably not be one of them. Ask her previous caretakers what and when they've been feeding her so you can maintain a consistent regimen and avoid any unnecessary stomach upset in the first week. Check with your vet if phasing in a new diet would be beneficial, and learn how to read dog food labels and what nutritional information to look for.

Whether your dog is allegedly housetrained or not, be prepared to spend a fair amount of time working with him on this, since a new environment can cause confusion. As soon as you get home for the first time, take him directly to where he will be expected to relieve himself, and continue to take him out with extra frequency for the first week or so to avoid accidents.

If you're going to be using a crate, make sure your dog has free access in and out while you're in the house so he can associate the crate with a safe place instead of confinement or punishment.

PETS

AND THE CITY

According to the Trust for Public Land, dog parks are currently the fastest growing segment of city parks. If Rover plays well with other pups off-leash, these urban oases offer a super opportunity for both human and canine exercise and social interaction. Check with your local municipality about dog parks in your area.

Some things to keep in mind:

• Bring your own water and bowl to reduce the risk of canine contagions.
• There's no such thing as the Poop Fairy. Always pick up after your pooch.
• You can only be responsible for your own dog, and others may not be responsible at all. Educate yourself about the potential risks of dog parks and interactive play.

THE PLAYGROUND AROUND TOWN

No dog parks nearby? Or your furry buddy is a bit squeamish (or too rough) to play with other dogs? Living in the city doesn't have to inhibit exercise or playtime. Making the urban landscape your obstacle course enables dogs and dog walkers to get more bang for their buck where there are fewer areas to walk. Weave around trees or light poles, jump up on benches, jog the front steps of a nearby building, and just get active!

ACCLIMATION & TRAINING

As excited as you and your household may be about welcoming a new member, try to take things easy and quiet for the first few days, especially if your dog is a more timid type, to allow him time to get used to the idea that this is his home too, and these are his people. You may also want to keep him in one room or general area for the first couple days to keep him from feeling overwhelmed in a new, large place.

Immediately starting a reliable daily routine is an excellent way to abate your dog's anxiety. A new setting and new family for her means that she has no idea what to expect next, so by making mealtimes, potty times, and bedtime predictable, it will help keep her calm.

Teaching your dog through positive reinforcement requires a lot of treats! Make sure you have kibble-sized rewards so you don't wind up overfeeding him over the course of his training. Overfeeding leads to obesity in dogs, which can cause serious health issues, like diabetes and arthritis. Talk to your vet about the appropriate daily caloric intake for your dog, based on his size and lifestyle.

You may or may not have a sense of the living environment where your dog came from. It could have been abusive, neglectful, or full of triggers that led to bad experiences for your pooch. In the first weeks as you acclimate to one another, take note of what cues cause positive or negative reactions. Even objects that seem innocuous to you—like a dog collar, a broom, or the rolled up morning paper—could possibly evoke an unexpected reaction from your rescue dog.

If you already have other dogs at home, make sure their first meeting with the new member of the family is on neutral territory, like a park or a friend's home. Keep them leashed by two separate individuals at first, in case they need to be quickly separated. Don't try to force them together if they're not showing any interest in one another, but be calm and use an upbeat tone of voice to cast the initial meeting as a positive experience. Above all, be patient with all your animals as they adapt to the change.

If your new dog is coming home to resident cats, the introduction should take place at home, but with a few preliminary days of separation before the meeting. Rotate which animals are confined to certain areas so they can get accustomed to each other's scent. When introductions are finally made, make sure your dog is leashed to see how both behave before letting them interact freely together. Whenever you're not in the house, they should also be separated to avoid a potential "cat-astrophe" in your absence. Check out the Resources section for more tips!

Consistency is key with your new rescue dog. Try not to give mixed signals by letting her think a behavior is acceptable, then showing her it's not, or vice versa. Use clear, simple verbal cues consistently to help build her vocabulary and solidify what certain words mean. You'll also want to make training easy and achievable, then increase the difficulty as she learns in increments.

DOGGONE FISHIN'

If you're a pro angler or just enjoy the sport of fishing, bringing Bubba along can be an enjoyable activity to share, provided he's well-behaved and won't be more effort to catch than the fish. If you plan on fishing in a public park area, make sure dogs are allowed. If you'll be in a boat, outfit Bubba with a life jacket and give him plenty of potty breaks on dry land. Don't forget to bring drinking water, treats, poop bags, and a leash (I promise you'll need them).

Dogs want to do the right thing and please their owner, so it's important to set the stage so they can build their confidence and their comprehension of what you're asking of them.

Be prepared to supervise your dog in the first few weeks more than you typically would after everyone has adjusted. Be wary of household items and finishes in reach of scratching, chewing, ingesting, or any other destructive behaviors. Try to keep as many of these objects as possible away from your dog. For those that can't be taken away, be diligent in monitoring for unwanted behavior and correct it immediately by redirecting his attention using positive reinforcement. Teaching a dog only what is unacceptable without helping him understand what is acceptable will result in a continual guessing game for him and set him up for failure.

If your new rescue is demonstrating aggression toward other animals in your home, or vice versa, your best bet is to seek professional advice from a trainer or behaviorist, rather than trying to figure out a solution on your own. It's important to understand what's triggering the behavior and how to address it so that it doesn't escalate in the future.

Dogs' exercise needs vary, based on age, breed, temperament, and so forth. As you get to know your dog, make sure you're providing sufficient regular activity, which will reduce boredom and destructive behavior. Multiple daily walks are necessary for most dogs. Even if you're not physically able to exercise your dog as much as necessary, or if the weather isn't cooperating, there are plenty of indoor activities that will get your dog's heartrate up without your own heart giving out. Try playing fetch or tug-of-war as a healthy substitute, if your dog is eager to participate.

"If there are no dogs in Heaven, then when I die I want to go where they went."

WILL ROGERS

5 COOL APPS FOR YOUR #SOCIALMEDIADOG

Why let Grumpy Cat® have all the fun? Take to your social media platform of choice and share with the world all the hilarious shenanigans and feats of adorableness that Molly Magoo performs daily. All you need is Internet access and a pair of opposable thumbs. Give these five a try, just for starters!

- ☐ DOGGYDATEZ
- ☐ MAPMYDOGWALK
- ☐ BARKCAM
- ☐ DOG BOOGIE
- ☐ INSTAGRAM (#DOGSOFINSTAGRAM)

If your dog is prone to taking you for a walk, instead of the other way around, one of the first steps to curtailing this behavior happens before the walk even begins. If he's acting hyper while you're putting the leash on him, stop and wait until he can sit or stand calmly before continuing with your walk routine. If he starts getting over-energized again, take another pause and wait for him to calm back down to a level of appropriate behavior—consistency is essential for this training to work. Though the process may take a while, controlling the tone of prepping for a walk will help you set the pace for the walk itself.

Leash devices like head halters and harnesses are also useful if your dog is a persistent puller during walks. They're harder to slip out of than collars, which can also damage a dog's trachea when pulling. Be sure to only move forward when there is slack in the leash, so your dog isn't pulling. As soon as he reaches the end of the slack, the walk should stop until he sits and redirects his attention to you. As soon as he does, you can resume the walk. Using a key word like "Look" as soon as he looks at you will help him learn to respond to you. Though the distance covered may be very short until your dog catches on, learning proper walking behavior is well worth the effort.

Walks are great opportunities to continue your obedience training, so remember to bring treats with you to reward appropriate walking behavior. While on a walk, be mindful of what your dog decides to put in his mouth and where he wanders, since landscaped areas can be treated with toxins, and certain flora and fauna are poisonous to dogs.

GO TAKE A HIKE

Depending on how close you are to the great outdoors, taking your dog on hiking trails is a fun way to spend quality time and to decompress after a stressful week. Make sure you have a good sense whether your dog can walk off-leash uneventfully, since other hikers, dogs and critters may surprise you on the trail. Also adhere to any local leash laws. Protection from ticks and insects is another must, and of course, don't forget your poop bags!

If walking through a buggy area, never spray your dog with insect repellant meant for humans, since they can face severe neurological complications from the ingredient DEET. Instead, ask your vet for dog-safe bug spray.

Picking up after your dog is a common courtesy in any community, no matter how rural. It's also an important sanitary measure, since feces attract pests and pestilence. Even if you'll only be going out for a quick jaunt, always have a couple of poop bags handy. It seems to be Murphy's Law that, the moment you're caught without one, your dog will make you wish you weren't.

On excursions that are longer than a stroll around the block, remember to bring plenty of water for both you and your dog, especially during the warmer months. Your dog doesn't sweat, but he can become dehydrated by panting to cool himself down. When traveling to places where other dogs will be, consider bringing your own water dish to keep your dog from catching any germs from sharing.

HEALTH, SAFETY & HYGIENE

Get in the habit of giving your dog a quick daily inspection of her body so you can establish what lumps and anomalies have been there since you got her, and which may be more recent. This includes checking for ticks, skin irritations, growths, sensitive areas, and any other troublesome issues. Check in her mouth, ears, under her coat, and between paw pads to be thorough.

If your dog is sensitive to being handled in general or touched on certain parts of his body, it could be for many different reasons. However, it is best to figure out why and begin working through the issue right away, instead of simply avoiding touching or handling him. Proceed with caution and take baby steps when determining how comfortable your dog is with being touched or handled, especially his mouth. Make sure you have a clear understanding of dog body language so you can be on the alert for any changes that show that your dog is getting uncomfortable, nervous or aggressive.

If you feel that your dog might bite you or someone else from his uneasiness, get a behaviorist involved, rather than putting yourself or others in jeopardy. Never force your dog to be handled if it's clear he's uncomfortable, since this will usually aggravate him further. If the behavior doesn't seem to be improving over time, seek assistance from your vet to rule out any medical issues, and potentially contact a behaviorist or trainer to explore desensitization or counterconditioning.

Grooming is a necessary part of dog ownership that most dogs aren't naturally fond of. Associate positive things with grooming times and always take it slowly and gently. If your dog has had bad grooming experiences in the past, you may have to be patient as you work through any fears or anxieties. Take it in stages to get him comfortable with each step of the process.

Brushing your dog regularly is a good way to keep him free of tangles and things that cling on from the outdoors. It also gives you a chance to inspect for insects like fleas and ticks, sensitive spots, and any bodily anomalies that may require medical attention.

As long as your dog isn't getting filthy on a regular basis, most dogs only need to be bathed a few times a year. Excessive bathing can strip them of their natural oils and lead to skin irritations or flaking. Consult your vet on the best bathing frequency for your dog, as well as a recommended mild shampoo that's specially formulated for dogs. Be sure to rinse really well!

Teeth brushing is also an important health regimen for your dog, just as it is for you. Try to brush your dog's teeth with dog-specific toothpaste a few times a week. If she's sensitive to having her muzzle handled, try getting her accustomed in stages; start by getting her used to having her mouth touched, then eventually introduce the toothbrush, then brushing with dog-formulated toothpaste. If your dog has bad breath, seek assistance from your vet. Various types of bad breath could indicate a dental concern or deeper medical issue.

Just like people need annual checkups by the doctor to stay healthy, so too does your dog. Find a vet in your area that comes recommended and that you and your dog feel comfortable with, and get your dog on a regular schedule. Building a medical history is also instrumental in effectively treating future issues.

Heartworm is a common canine malady, though it's easily preventable. Heartworm is spread only by the bite of an infected mosquito; it's not contagious between dogs, and people can't contract it. Inquire with your shelter or rescue if your dog has been on heartworm preventative treatments or if she has been tested while in their care. If she tests positive, you'll need to start her immediately on a rigorous treatment, since the disease is fatal if left untreated. Even if your dog tests negative, talk to your vet about starting a heartworm preventative regimen, which is inexpensive and easy to administer. Then be sure to get your dog tested for heartworm every spring to help her stay parasite-free.

One of the best ways to keep animals out of shelters, besides adopting, is spaying or neutering your dog. The procedures not only help lower the number of homeless animals, but they have also been proven to reduce the risk of certain cancers in animals, as well as improve or eliminate some undesirable behaviors, such as roaming, marking, irritability, and aggression.

According to the ASPCA (American Society for the Prevention of Cruelty to Animals), you should never feed your dog any of the following items, which can pose serious health risks and may even be fatal if ingested:

ALCOHOL
AVOCADO
EGGS
GRAPES OR RAISINS
MACADAMIA NUTS
MILK
RAW OR UNDERCOOKED MEAT, EGGS AND BONES
ONIONS OR CHIVES
POULTRY BONES (THEY SPLINTER)
CHOCOLATE
COFFEE (OR ANYTHING CAFFEINATED)
SALTY FOODS
TOMATO LEAVES, STEMS OR UNRIPE TOMATOES
YEAST DOUGH
MOLDY OR SPOILED FOOD
XYLITOL (A COMMONLY USED SWEETENER)
ANY MEDICATIONS NOT SPECIFICALLY PRESCRIBED TO YOUR DOG

Buckling up isn't just the law, it's the best way to keep your dog safe in the car. Dogs should only ride in the back seat, like children, since airbag deployment could injure or kill them. They should also be restrained by a device specifically designed for them in transit—sitting in your lap is unsafe for both of you, no matter how small your dog is. Additionally, even though it looks cute and your dog may love it, allowing her to stick her head out of the window when the car is in motion is a dangerous practice, since she could be thrown from the vehicle in an accident.

Depending on the size and strength of your dog, jumping up on people in excitement can be anything from a nuisance to a serious liability, especially if children or infirm adults are around. Be consistent in teaching your dog that jumping on people is unacceptable, regardless of the person— your dog won't be the best at differentiating who can be jumped on safely and who can't. Before someone approaches your dog, ask the person to wait and hand them a treat. Ask your dog to sit and stay seated as the greeter comes over. If your dog manages to stay seated, let the greeter reward him with a treat and scratch under his chin. If he stands or jumps up, have the greeter stay out of reach of your dog and ignore him while withholding the treat. Try again until your dog can say hello without jumping up.

15 FUN ATHLETIC ACTIVITIES

Get outside for some fresh air romps—or find some awesome indoor facilities—and revel in the open spaces you and your pup can explore! Turn the page for more information on each bucket list item!

- ☐ GIVE IT A TREIBBALL!
- ☐ DO THE DOWNTOWN DOGGY-PADDLE
- ☐ TEACH HAND TARGETING
- ☐ GO DOCK DIVING
- ☐ PLAY FLYBALL IN TEAMS OF FOUR
- ☐ TRY CANINE MUSICAL FREESTYLE
- ☐ PLAY ULTIMATE FRISBEE
- ☐ GO SKIJORING TOGETHER

- ☐ DO THE FOUR-LEGGED DASH— A HUMAN-VERSUS-DOG RUNNING RACE!
- ☐ PLAY A GAME OF TUG-OF-WAR
- ☐ GO CROSS-COUNTRY SKIING
- ☐ GO CANOEING OR KAYAKING
- ☐ TAKE A SNOWSHOEING EXCURSION
- ☐ GIVE STAND-UP PADDLE BOARDING A TRY
- ☐ MAKE ROLLERBLADING COOL AGAIN

15 ACTIVITIES FOR THE SPORTY DOG

Give It a Treibball!

The sport of Treibball (pronounced TRY-ball), enables dogs and handlers alike to play together while promoting better teamwork and communication through classic obedience and herding cues.

Do the Downtown Doggy-Paddle

For dogs (or humans) with arthritis or joint conditions, dog-friendly swimming facilities are perfect for low-impact activity that delivers a total-body workout.

Right on Target

Hand targeting teaches canine focus by training your dog to touch your hand on command. It serves as a helpful technique in a variety of circumstances, such as when your dog is nervous, distracted, misbehaving, frightened, or getting too aggressive. Hand targeting is also used in agility training, where dogs navigate obstacles. Visit the ASPCA website for guidance on teaching your dog to hand target.

Take the Plunge

Dock diving, also known as dock jumping, is a competitive sport that measures the height and/or distance your dog can jump into a body of water off a dock in pursuit of a toy. If you and your dog really get into the spirit, organizations such as DockDogs, Splash Dogs, and Ultimate Air Dogs offer the chance to join clubs and register in competitions.

With Flying Colors

In flyball, dogs in teams of fours relay race over a series of hurdles to a springboard at the far end of the course. Each racer jumps on the springboard, which shoots out a tennis ball that the dog has to catch. The dog then races back over the hurdles to the handler, setting off the next runner on the team. Watching seasoned flyball athletes in action is truly impressive, and the dogs' enthusiasm is evident.

No One Puts Puppy in a Corner

Canine Musical Freestyle is the combination of obedience training, dog tricks, and choreography, where a handler and a dog perform a dance routine to music. National and international organizations offer membership, classes and competitions for those up to the challenge. Not a fan of audiences? You can still turn up Springsteen and have a great time with Chance, even if you're just dancin' in the bark.

"Buddy, Get Big!"

Take a contemporary twist on an old favorite and introduce Scamp to a game of Ultimate Frisbee. Once your dog has mastered some obedience commands and Frisbee basics (admittedly, throwing may not be his strong suit), let him join you and your pals in an orchestrated game with a disc that's made for dogs. Get ready to mark your man, block a Scoober, huck that disc down field, and watch your canine Landshark get big on the Universe Point.

Row, Row, Row Your Dog

Canoeing and kayaking can be relaxing or exhilarating water sports that you and Gizmo might enjoy together, as long as everyone is well prepared. No matter what, first consult with experts who have paddled with dogs before to ensure your safety and your dog's.

On Your Barks, Get Set, Snow!

In Skijoring, a harnessed dog or dogs pull a cross-country skier through a course, as the skier propels himself forward. The dogs add an extra speed and endurance component to the race. Even if you're skijoring just for fun, it's a great winter activity for high-energy dogs with strong focus and who weigh at least 35 pounds.

Get Pulled In

A game of tug-of-war with your pup makes for excellent entertainment and exercise, relieving pent-up energy that might otherwise get misdirected. It gives your dog a legitimate and safe way to use his or her teeth, while building a healthy relationship with you. Tug-of-war can also serve as a distraction from unwanted behavior or as a confidence-booster in timid dogs.

The Four-Legged Dash

If your dog loves to run and has mastered the heel and release commands, a human-versus-dog running race is an exciting way to add a little competition to outdoor playtime, if you're up for the challenge. Many dog breeds and mixes love to be chased, which is likely what you'll be doing in a cloud of Bandit's dust, once he gets the hang of it!

Get in the Glide Zone

Cross-country skiing is a fantastic way for both you and your canine to stay active through the cold winters. Though Rusty won't be strapping a pair of Nordic skis to his paws, he will enjoy keeping up with your stride, if you trust him off-leash.

Paddle with Your Pup

Stand-up paddle boarding can be as exerting or relaxing as you like, and what's more, Rocky can join you! Make sure you acclimate your dog on dry land first, then gradually in the water so that she doesn't panic and listens to sit/stay commands. Get a very stable board, since it will have to support both of you, and figure out where on the board is the safest spot for your dog to be, depending on her size. As with any water sport, always equip your dog with a life preserver, bring plenty of water for both of you, and slather any short-haired sun-sensitive areas with a sunscreen designed for dogs.

Bring Back the 'Blades!

Face it, there's a part of you that misses the '90s, when you were rocking out to your Discman, and rollerblading was as cool as frosted tips. Why should it all be relinquished to the past? Dust off your old inline skates or spring for a new pair (yes, they still sell them) and bring Duke alongside for a roll down Memory Lane.

Buddy in the Backcountry

As with other winter sports, snowshoeing with your dog can be a highly enjoyable time for both of you. Remember to outfit him properly for the cold, bring a leash and plenty of snacks and water for both of you, and monitor your pooch for exhaustion and hypothermia. With safety precautions squared away, you're ready to hit the trail!

A DOG BEHAVIOR PRIMER FOR THE TWO-LEGGED

For us mere humans, animal cues and behavior can be complicated to decipher. Even if you've grown up with animals in your home or on a farm, it's not hard for the occasional message to get lost in translation when the communicating parties don't share the same language—or species, for that matter. (And you thought the dating scene was hard!) Thanks to specialists who have spent lifetimes decoding the meanings behind dog behaviors and interactions, people can interpret these basic cues and behaviorisms to get a better idea of what a dog is thinking or feeling and react appropriately.

Smiling

It's not just an internet meme or the latest CGI trick in an *Air Bud* movie; smiling or grinning is an actual canine behavior that some people mistake for bearing teeth in an aggressive or threatening manner. Depending on the environment and the dog's other body language, he may be trying to communicate quite the opposite by showing submission, sometimes anxiously, to that animal or person. (Think of coming home to chewed shoes or a decimated wastepaper basket. When you confront Spot hiding under the bed, you may find him simpering back at you.)

In cases where smiling receives positive reinforcement, such as a belly rub or a treat from a human who finds it to be adorable, the dog may learn to smile intentionally as a means of getting rewarded … or avoiding punishment.

Showing Aggression

One of the ways to know whether a dog is smiling or snarling is loud and clear—if he's making any growling sounds, you're going to want to back off immediately and cautiously. If he isn't growling, but is showing fangs, puckering his muzzle, wrinkling his forehead, tensing his body, or breathing heavily, these are also the signals to back away. Other more subtle cues of aggression include ears back, tail low, lips pulled tautly over teeth, and a direct stare.

YOU'RE HIRED!

Just like humans, lots of dogs feel happier when they have a sense of purpose. Give Buster a job—one that he enjoys and he's good at—to make him feel needed and purposeful. Jobs can be as simple as having him wear a doggy pack of unused poop bags and other necessary items while you're out on your walks, or teaching him to shut the door behind him when you come in from outside. Get creative on simple ways he can help out, and be sure to "pay" him a fair wage in treats!

Feeling Relaxed

Dogs that are relaxed will generally take on—well—a relaxed appearance. Their muscles will not be tensed, their weight will be evenly balanced, and their tail and ears will be in their natural positions—tail up, ears forward. When a dog is at ease, his mouth may be closed or slightly open, sometimes with the corners very slightly turned upward, or perhaps panting gently. His facial expressions and body stances will not look strained or assertive, and his eyes will appear normal-sized and placid, with little to none of the whites showing.

Playing

Playfulness in dogs is usually easy to spot through upbeat, bouncy movements, though some humans can confuse well-intentioned boisterousness for aggression or malice. Downward-Facing Dog is not just a yoga pose, but also the universal canine symbol for "Let's play!" This is often referred to as the play bow, where the dog lowers his head and forelegs to the ground and raises his hindquarters in the air. Dogs use this move to signal to animals and humans that any roughhousing to follow is not meant in a harmful way, since adult dog and puppy play can sometimes be characterized by nips, pounces, high energy, and even faux growls and barks.

Feeling Anxious

Anxiety or nervousness can be a transitional phase between feeling relaxed and showing aggression, since a dog's fear may cause her to lash out if she feels threatened. It's therefore important for people to understand their dog's anxiety, what triggers it, and how to keep it from escalating into something more serious.

Though humans tend to yawn when they're tired or bored, dog yawning is more often a behavior that reflects submission or anxiety in stressful situations, rather than fatigue. It's meant to send a peacemaking message to the perceived threat to avoid or displace conflict. You may choose to observe and document what causes your dog to yawn to help mitigate her stress as it occurs.

Panting can be another sign of anxiety in dogs, depending on the circumstance, since dogs will also pant to cool themselves down after exertion or in warm weather. Always take the behavior in context. If a dog is panting heavily, abruptly stops, and exhibits other aggressive mannerisms described above, like pinned ears or a tensed body—back away. She may have transitioned from fear to aggression and could be preparing to snap at you.

When a dog fixes her gaze, but turns her head away slightly, exposing the whites of her eyes, this is commonly referred to as whale eye, and it can be a sign of anxiety. Again, take the behavior in context and look for any other indicators of stress or aggression. Play it safe by backing away until the dog's demeanor becomes more relaxed.

THE SWIFTER SNIFFER

Your dog's sense of smell is anywhere between 10,000 to 100,000 times stronger than yours. Put Spot's sniffer to the test with scent games to help hone his honker while making great rainy day entertainment for you both. Games like Which-Hand-is-the-Treat-in and Find-the-Kibble-in-the-Dark are just a few of many progressively more difficult variations on the same concept. Go with the tried-and-true games, or come up with some on your own! When treats are involved, your dog will definitely want to play along.

Urinating

Besides having a full bladder, there are several reasons why a dog may be urinating at inopportune times. Puppies and non-housetrained dogs are still gaining control of their bladders, so taking them out frequently to relieve themselves is the best way to keep the wee off your floor. It's also best to rule out medical reasons for inappropriate urination by taking your dog to the vet. In other circumstances, you may find that your dog is urinating when excited, such as at play or in greetings. Try taking playtime outside and keeping greetings calm by avoiding high-pitched voices or stimulating contact, such as hugging and roughhousing.

Puppies and timid adult dogs may also use urination as a display of submission, in response to loud noises, arguments, or if they feel like they're getting reprimanded. This behavior is sometimes accompanied by submissive postures, such as exposing the belly, tail-tucking, crouching, and trying to look small. Be patient and never scold your dog for submissive urination, as it will typically only increase the behavior.

Marking is another type of urination your dog might exhibit on walks, in the yard, in your home, or in someone else's. Both male and female dogs can mark for different reasons, such as coming into heat, responding to social or environmental triggers, and experiencing anxiety, among others. The ASPCA offers insight on how to address unwanted marking. Check out the Resources section for details.

Regardless of the reason behind unwanted urination behavior, use positive reinforcement, like praise and treats when your dog does the right thing. Never yell, hit, scold or intimidate your dog for urinating, and eliminate residual urine odors to remove familiar cues to repeat the behavior.

Poop Eating

And you thought peeing in the house was bad! Some dogs will indeed engage in this behavior, medically referred to as *Coprophagia*. (If you have to talk about it in public, you might want to use the scientific term!) Vets and behaviorists have different theories on why dogs do this, and much depends on your dog's temperament and history.

It's possible that your dog simply has a repugnant habit you will need to help break, or he may be feeling bored or looking for attention. He might also actually like the smell and taste of poop; dogs ancestrally would scavenge for anything they could to survive, so this is not totally out of the norm.

Mother dogs may also attempt to clean up their den to avoid attracting predators. In a group of dogs, if one is sick, a healthy dog might try to cover up the evidence to predators that one of the pack mates is in a weakened state. Dogs that are lower in the hierarchy of a group of

"A barking dog
is often more useful
than a sleeping lion."

WASHINGTON IRVING

dogs might also present this behavior to demonstrate their submission. If your dog came from a situation where he was underfed, he may have resorted to eating feces and continued to do so out of habit, even now that he's getting fed regularly. Dogs will also instinctively try to replace missing enzymes and nutrients from their digestive tract if they're not getting what they need from their diet, or if they aren't able to absorb it normally.

Head Cocking

This is one of the more adorable dog behaviors, because there's something so humanlike about it. While the definitive reason is unknown, behaviorists tend to believe that when a dog cocks his head, he's trying to make sense of what you're saying or what's going on. He may be waiting for cues to help clue him in to your next move or what his should be. He might also not be sure where a sound is coming from, like if you squeak a toy that's out of sight.

As with any excessive behavior, consult your vet if your dog is holding his head to one side more often than you'd expect with the normal reasons for head tilting.

ROAD DAWGZ

Plan to see the country one campground at a time? No one will make a more enthusiastic companion than Spike. Rent an RV for all the comforts of home on the road while you're between parks or camp sites. Just make sure the places you visit are dog-friendly and that you've beefed up on all the rules before heading out. Next stop: The World's Largest Bottle of Catsup! (… Located in Collinsville, Illinois, if you're interested.)

Butt Sniffing

Perhaps one of the most common behaviors associated with dogs (it turns out to be an undesirable trait in people), butt-sniffing is a dog's way of walking up to a new dog, shaking hands, and exchanging business cards. According to the American Chemical Society, it is actually a chemical form of communication that reveals important information immediately about a dog's gender, immune system, reproductive status, diet, current emotional state, and other tidbits that humans might find on Facebook.

Tail Chasing

This is another dog behavior that, when exhibited in people, means something entirely else! But the variation your dog may present is one that can be as benign as her trying to use up some excess energy.

However, it can also be symptomatic of something that requires your attention, such as anal glands that need to be expressed or an allergy or parasite causing itching. If you notice your dog dragging her rear across the floor repeatedly, licking her own butt, or chewing her tail, consult your vet about the behavior.

Other reasons for tail chasing can be psychological, such as a compulsion disorder, which can occur for many different reasons. Compulsive behavior can also manifest in many different ways, not just tail chasing. Journaling your pup's repetitive behavior regularly with as many details as possible and consulting your vet is the best course of action if the behavior persists.

Hiding Food

Does your dog act more like a squirrel facing the onset of winter? Does she take bits of kibble and "hide" them around the house? The usual reason for this isn't too far off. Dogs will instinctively hide their food when it's plentiful so there will be something to eat on the less reliable days or seasons. Unfortunately, Trixie doesn't understand you're going to give her another bowl tomorrow. Food left around the house may seem cute at first, but it can attract pests and start to stink if undiscovered for a while. Your dog might also try to "bury" it in your richly upholstered sofa or your newly finished hardwood floors and wind up ruining parts of your home.

To lessen the anxiety that accompanies your dog's uncertainty or anticipation, start a consistent mealtime regimen for her. This routine can include a walk before meals to release excess energy. Before placing a bowl of food in front of your dog, require that she sit and remain calm before being rewarded with her food dish so she learns that being rambunctious is not acceptable, particularly at mealtimes. When she complies, give her the food. If she walks away from her dish while there is still food in it, pick up the dish and hang onto it out of her sight in case she gets hungry later. This will ensure she's eating enough without stashing leftovers in your corners or cushions.

DOUBLE THE LOVE

So you've rescued T-Bone, and he's now safe in a loving home. Success! But if you still have that nagging urge to help other dogs out there, fostering can be an excellent form of assistance that you and your rescue can do together, provided no one is dog aggressive. Not only will you be giving another dog in need a wonderful place to stay as they wait to find their forever home, but your own pup could benefit from having a buddy around to keep him company and work on socialization skills.

Mounting

It doesn't matter if your dog is male or female, or if he or she has intact reproductive organs; mounting (or humping) is more than just a sexual behavior for dogs. This can be a display of dominance, excitement, or demonstrate a lack of adequate socialization.

Since mounting can make for an embarrassing day at the dog park, you'll want to discourage your dog from doing it, but without punishing him. Tell him to stop or get up and walk away if you're the immediate object of his affection. Separate your dog from others who are on the receiving end. If your dog has a particular pillow or inanimate object he practices this on, you might even let him have at it, once in a while, if the behavior is not extreme. As with any excessive behavior, if you're concerned it may be indicating a medical issue, consult your vet.

MUDDY MUTTS

If you're the down-and-dirty type with a truck and a swath of muddy farm land, you and Spot can get spotty all over in a good ol' mud bogging outing. Just make sure your dog already enjoys riding in vehicles, and that all participants are safely secured for the all-terrain slippery conditions. Hose downs for everyone afterward!

Digging Indoors

As mentioned earlier, hiding food can be accompanied by digging indoors, in attempt to "bury" food for later. Dogs might also do this with their "treasures," like favorite toys, a bone, etc.

Additionally, dogs will dig at the carpet, furniture or flooring in an instinctive attempt to make a comfortable den to lie down in (even if the laminate flooring doesn't appear to be getting any fluffier.) Dogs will usually accompany this behavior with circling a few times to tread out a bed for themselves. Your dog might also be trying to get warm or cool off by digging, either indoors or outdoors, or he may simply be amusing himself.

According to the ASPCA, digging can be an indicator of anxiety or a desire to escape, depending on the situation. Of course, even benign reasons for digging can still result in unwanted damage to your home. You'll need to understand the impetus for the behavior to figure out the best method for discouraging or eliminating it, especially if the digging is indicating distress. If the behavior is anxiety related, focus on removing stressors or helping your dog feel calmer in those situations. Consult a behaviorist or your vet, if necessary.

Chewing

Puppies, like teething infants, will often chew things to help their gums feel better as their teeth come in. This is also how they learn about their world, the same way babies love to put things in their mouths.

In adult dogs, there can be many reasons for chewing, including boredom, anxiety, attention-seeking, or never having been taught that chewing is inappropriate, among other reasons. Understand that he's not chewing your new Louboutin pumps as a personal vendetta for making him go pee-pee in the rain earlier.

If you find the remains of a chewed object after the fact, don't punish your dog—he's already unaware that the shoes he chewed hours ago equate to an unwanted behavior, and he'll have a hard time learning from the experience. If you catch him in the act, sternly tell him "No" and take away whatever he's chewing, always replacing it with an appropriate chew toy. Be sure to praise him once his attention is on his toy, so he learns what items are okay to chew.

Continue to set your dog up for success by making his chew toys easily distinguishable from non-toys, redirecting his attention to his toys with excitement, and keeping the things you don't want chewed out of reach. You'll also want to keep a watchful eye on him until he begins to learn. Just remember to never hit or yell at him.

Fear of Thunder and Fireworks

Ever find your dog cowering in the bathtub or under a table during a rainstorm or on the Fourth of July? Loud noises like thunder and fireworks can be terrifying to dogs, since they don't understand the science of lightning bolts and sound waves, or the human obsession with colorful explosives. All they know is those loud noises represent a threat coming to get them and, *for crying out loud, why are you not under this table with me?!*

SHORE TO PLEASE

Romping on a sandy patch of shoreline in the off-season or on days with fewer beachgoers is often a crowd pleaser among canines, on- or off-leash. Check ahead to make sure your destination beach is dog-friendly for the season when you'll be visiting, and always leave the sand and surf as you (hopefully) found it—litter- and dog poop-free. Fetch toys are a smart item to bring, and sun protection and plenty of drinking water for both of you are must-haves, even on overcast days. Now get out there and chase some seagulls!

"All knowledge,
the totality of all
questions and all answers,
is contained in the dog."

FRANZ KAFKA

While you can't stop thunder from clapping or communities from making merry with fireworks on a summer evening, there are a few things you can do to make your dog feel better. According to The Humane Society of the United States, letting her find her "safe place" is key. If she doesn't have access to this spot, try to give her access; if it's not okay for her to go there, try providing another small, dark spot with easy in-and-out access for her, which she views as safe. Never try to confine her in a safe place against her will, since this will bring on more anxiety.

If you have white noise available to you, like a fan, a vent, or even music, try putting those on to mask some of the scary sounds. You might also try distracting your dog with a game and treats. Some important things NOT to do include confining your dog in her crate or any other space where she doesn't have the freedom to enter and exit, punishing her, or trying to desensitize her to the scary sounds by forcing her to experience them more acutely.

A counterintuitive thing some behaviorists say NOT to do is to reassure your dog with cuddles, treats, petting, baby talk, etc. While it's in our nature to try to soothe a frightened animal or child, the animal may interpret our behavior as reinforcement for their own fearfulness instead of reassurance that there's no reason to be afraid. The frightening stimulus may still scare them, in spite of any calming efforts.

However, it's worth noting that another school of thought believes comforting your dog is a positive thing to do during thunder or fireworks. Whether you plan on ignoring the noises or comforting your dog through them, a great stress reducer for your dog is to simply be in your presence.

Dogs are such characters, especially when their personalities are fostered in loving, nurturing homes. Whatever the behaviorism in your dog that you wish to decipher or remedy, remember to take detailed notes as the behavior occurs, consider things from a dog's perspective, get curious with your research, and don't be shy to seek advice from a vet or behaviorist if the issue becomes troublesome.

BUCKET LIST

FIVE ORGANIZED ACTIVITIES FOR ANY ATHLETE OR COUCH POTATO (HUMAN OR CANINE!)

You can be a triathlete or a dedicated fan, and still enjoy the thrill of sports and games! Jump in with your rescue dog and feel the burn—or the couch!

☐ **BUILD AN AGILITY COURSE— FOR BOTH OF YOU TO COMPLETE!**

☐ **WALK IN A PARADE WITH YOUR POOCH**

☐ **TAIL-GATE A LOCAL GAME TOGETHER**

☐ **WATCH THE PUPPY BOWL ON ANIMAL PLANET**

☐ **GO TO A BASEBALL GAME AT A PET-FRIENDLY VENUE**

——

THE RESCUE DOG'S BAG OF TRICKS

Learning a new trick is an accomplishment that both you and your dog can take pride in, not to mention that the process itself can be an amusing and rewarding bonding experience. Some tricks will wow onlookers, and others will elicit adoring "awwws."

In addition to making for great showmanship, tricks can be useful tools for helping your dog focus when it's necessary and respond to your cues. Other benefits include practical applications, like obeying commands that keep them out of danger, building their confidence when approaching new things, and offering them a source of mental stimulation.

Before attempting to teach your puppy or your old dog a new trick, it's important to ensure she's healthy enough and physically able and willing to do what you're asking. Some movements might be uncomfortable or taxing for a dog with medical or age-related limitations, so always keep your pooch's condition in mind, especially if she seems to have pronounced difficulty with the trick.

PORCHING IT

A pleasant way to enjoy the warm weather while staying cool and relaxed is hanging out on your porch, patio, balcony, or front stoop with a glass of something refreshing for you and your buddy to drink. Rock on the porch swing together, watch dogs walk by with their humans, or enjoy some music in the company of your pal.

It's also important to understand that teaching tricks requires even more patience from you than your dog. If she starts to lose interest or feel flustered after repeat failed attempts, find a positive note to end on (even the tiniest of things), reward her with a treat, and call it quits before the trick-teaching experience becomes an unpleasant one. Then try again later in the day. In general, teaching sessions should remain brief and always positive.

Above all, never punish or reprimand your dog for not performing the behavior you want from her. Remember that she doesn't speak your language any better than you speak hers, and for trick teaching to build a healthy relationship between the two of you, it's essential that you focus on positive reinforcement for desired behaviors and ignore unwanted behaviors.

If you're looking to challenge yourself and your dog to a little more than sit, stay, speak—all of which are necessary foundational disciplines that your dog will need to learn in order to accomplish harder ones—the following are several other tricks that are fun to learn and entertaining when mastered. If you're already familiar with clicker training, feel free to incorporate it into your trick teaching as reinforcement when your dog performs a desired behavior. Otherwise, simple verbal cues like "Yes" and "Good" can work just as well.

CLEAN UP YOUR ROOM

Your dog may be an expert when it comes to taking her toys out, but getting them back in their basket probably doesn't come as naturally. Luckily, there's a trick for that, which will make Fifi feel like it's just as fun to put her toys away as it is playing with them.

HOW TO DO IT:

1. Start with one toy on the floor and a basket or container a few feet away. Reinforce verbally or with clicks any interaction with the toy, then drop the treat in the basket for her to get.

2. Continue this a couple of times, then hold off on rewarding until your dog picks the toy up. Place the treat in the basket for her to eat, and repeat this process.

3. When your dog finally drops the first toy into the basket, give extra treats (commonly referred to as "jackpotting") to reinforce the behavior.

4. If your dog is taking a while to bring the toy to the basket on her own, try another approach by placing the basket directly in front of you and tossing her the toy, asking her to bring it back to you. Reward her for bringing it back, then begin holding off on rewards until she drops it in or near the basket.

5. Eventually, only reward her when the toy is dropped directly in the basket. Once your dog gets consistent with this, try going back to leaving the toy away from you, stationary on the floor, and asking her to retrieve it and bring it to the basket. Reward profusely for success or even near successes.

6. Once your dog gets consistent with putting a single toy away, after she does so, immediately place a new toy down with a treat beside it.

7. When she puts the second toy in the basket, reward with a treat beside a third toy put down in the last toy's place.

8. If your dog goes retrograde and tries to take any toys out of the basket, tell her to drop it and put a treat next to the toy waiting to be put away.

9. Keep putting out toys in succession with treats beside them until your dog really gets the hang of being rewarded for putting them in the basket. If you find that she starts to struggle with the concept again, try dropping a treat back in the basket to remind her of the point of the activity. Sometimes it's just a matter of waiting a bit for your dog to do what you want.

10. Start putting out two or three toys in a pile together with a treat next to them for encouragement. As your dog succeeds, add more toys to the pile.

11. When your dog automatically heads toward the next successive toy without needing an incentive, "jackpot" for this linked behavior. If you need to put another treat down beside the third toy afterward to keep her going, do so.

12. After she has linked a few toy placements, try rewarding at the completion of a different series of linked placements. She did two successive toys, now wait for three, then go back to rewarding two, then wait for four, etc. Gradually increase the criteria for rewards until you have asked her to successively put away the whole pile of toys unprompted. However, don't make the pile so big that she becomes disheartened or loses interest.

13. Finally, incorporate a verbal cue immediately before signaling for the desired behavior, such as "Clean up," "Clean your room" or "Put your toys away." Your dog should learn to associate the verbal cue with the performance, at which point you can take away the original cue to pick up her toys. Eventually, try varying the conditions, such as the distance to the basket, the location in the house, etc., so that your dog learns to do this uniformly.

THAT PUZZLED LOOK

Though sticks and tennis balls still make for tried-and-true dog entertainment, if you're looking for toys that challenge Rover's IQ (or simply keep him quietly occupied), rest assured there is a lucrative commercial market for that! Pet supply stores and online shopping platforms offer a ton of interactive dog toys, most of which are in the form of puzzles that unlock treats after much prodding and contemplation by your dog. One beloved classic is the KONG; others include the Tricky Treat Ball, the Busy Buddy Magic Mushroom, and yes, even the Dog Casino. But all bets are off if your pooch figures out how to operate the puzzle before you do.

WERE YOU RAISED IN A BARN? (SHUT THE FRONT DOOR!)

Unless you have a great doggy door, chances are you spend a lot of time playing porter at Chateau de Dogge (otherwise known as your home). Though you may have to open doors for your pampered pup, there's no reason why she can't learn to at least close them herself.

HOW TO DO IT:

1. Hold up a treat to the ajar door that you'd like closed, high enough for your dog to have to jump up on the door for it, while saying "Door" or "Close the door."

2. Have your dog continue to jump against the door until it closes all the way; only then should you give her the treat. If her jump attempts don't close the door all the way, keep saying "Door" and hold the treat in place, just out of her reach, until she succeeds in closing it completely.

3. Once your dog has mastered this stage, try pointing to the door with a treat in hand and saying "Door." If your dog isn't quite catching on, walk over to the door, hold the treat against it, while saying "Door," but then take it away before your dog jumps up, so she can get used to jumping on the door with no treat visible.

4. Reward her with the treat once she has shut the door all the way, without you holding the treat in front of her the whole time.

5. Finally, try to use the command "Door" or "Close the door" from afar. When she shuts the door, always be sure to give her the treat she expects.

NOTE: Keep in mind that, if you have beautiful doors that are not particularly scratch-resistant, you might not want your dog to get used to jumping on them. The choice is yours!

ONE PUPPY SHORT OF A PICNIC

Break out the red gingham blanket and sandwich fixin's! It's a glorious day to go for a picnic with Petey. Whether you live in the suburbs, the countryside, or the heart of a major city, a patch of public green space is bound to be nearby. Invite some friends along with their dogs and make an afternoon of it. If you're going to share food, just make sure Petey only eats the ones that are safe for him.

RING FOR A TINKLE

In the olden days, the poshest members of society rang for their servants ... which is how Mr. Bojangles will summon you when it's time for his morning constitutional.

 HOW TO DO IT:

1. Once your dog is housebroken, a useful trick is getting him to ring a bell to let you know when he needs to go out. However, until your dog understands the concept of relieving himself outdoors, this trick won't be very useful.

2. Start by putting a bell on the floor between you and your dog. It can be a cowbell on a lanyard or a bell you'd ring for service at a receptionist's desk. Whatever type of bell you prefer, just make sure it's durable, doesn't have any accessible parts a dog can swallow, and is easily ringable for your dog.

3. Get your dog interested in the bell by placing a treat against it. When he goes for the treat and touches the bell with his nose or paw, jackpot this behavior.

4. Once your dog is interested in the bell, only reward when he makes contact with it without treats already being beside it. Repeat this a few times until he comes to understand that making contact with the bell results in a treat. When he rings the bell, jackpot this as the specific desired behavior.

5. As you progress, begin only rewarding your dog when he rings the bell. This should eventually cue him to ring it to receive a treat.

6. Once he understands ringing the bell equals treats, place the bell by the door and lead your dog over. Allow him to try ringing the bell beside the door to get treats.

7. When it's time to take your dog out, ring the bell yourself and immediately put on his leash and take him outside to do his business. Repeat this every time you take him out, so he begins to associate the ringing bell with relieving himself.

8. After doing this several times, try pointing to the bell just before taking your dog out, so he realizes he can ring it himself and trigger going outside.

9. With enough repetition, your dog will begin to ring the bell himself when he feels the urge to go out. When he does this successfully, be sure to make a big fuss and give him lots of rewards. Just make sure the bell rings loudly enough that you can hear it when you're in another room.

NOTE: If your dog begins ringing the bell when you know he doesn't have to go out, be careful to not encourage excessive bell rings by letting him out when you're certain he doesn't have to go. Try to distract him for the moment by bringing him into another room and playing a game or capturing his attention another way.

"Dogs and philosophers
do the greatest good
and get the fewest
rewards."

DIOGENES

SING IT OUT

Help your dog channel his inner Justin Timberlake by teaching him to hit the high notes when singing along to your favorite tunes.

 HOW TO DO IT:

1. Have your dog seated in front of you as you teach him this trick. It's important to be very consistent with how and when you ask for this particular "singing" behavior, so your dog doesn't decide at an inopportune time that it's appropriate to howl or whine for a treat.

2. With a treat in your hand, try using visual and/or verbal cues, such as holding up your hands like a conductor about to start a symphony or saying something simple like, "Sing!"

3. If you hold your hands up with the treat and look away from your dog, he might begin to make noises to get your attention. As soon as he does this, even slightly, reward him and repeat the process, holding out for ever louder and longer vocalizations.

4. Try to encourage whatever type of sound you're looking for by rewarding those that come closest, such as a howl versus a bark, or a whine versus a growl. You may also want to reward different patterns of sounds to more closely resemble "singing." If you hold out a bit before giving him the treat, he'll probably try different nuances to figure out what will make you turn the reward over.

5. Eventually, the conductor hands and/or the "Sing" command will provoke him to vocalize on cue.

NOTE: This is a trick that may have a Dr. Frankenstein effect ... in other words, you might end up creating a monster. If you're not sure you want to encourage your dog to express himself so vocally (especially at 3:00 a.m., when he decides it's time to "sing,") consider holding off on this trick. Save it for mature dogs who understand the difference between performing on cue and simply making a scene.

YOU ARE GETTING SLEEPY, VERY ZZZLEEPY

Like kids, dogs do great with routines and schedules. Keeping relatively consistent wake-up, meal, and bedtimes provides reliable structure to each day and helps mitigate dog anxiety. Starting a sleeping routine, even if it doesn't occur at exactly the same time every night, is a good way to cue your dog that it's time for bed, and it may even help him sleep through the night better. Try using the same actions and phrases in the same order before hunkering down for the evening (like a final walk, a nighty-night snack, and a goodnight phrase before showing him to his bed). As Pavlov demonstrated a century ago, dogs are psychologically and physiologically highly adaptive to cues and routines. See how quickly Bruno catches on to your own nightly sequence!

SAYING PRAYERS

It's not just people who can count their blessings; you can teach Rover to say his prayers before bedtime.

HOW TO DO IT:

1. This trick is taught at the edge of the bed. First ensure that your dog is at a comfortable height where he'll be able to put both paws up and bow his head between his front legs.

2. With a treat, encourage your dog to put his paws up on the bed. If he gets one paw up, praise him and give him the treat. You might also give a verbal or clicker cue to let him know he got it right.

3. Repeat this process a few times until you can get him to put both paws up. If he's reluctant, put the treat under his nose and pull it toward the bed to motion him to bring the other paw up. When he does, reward him, give your cue, and repeat it until he fully understands what you're asking for.

4. Your dog is halfway there, but you now must get him to bow his head. With both paws on the bed, slowly lower the treat from above the bed to below the edge so his head follows the motion down. Let him know this is "Say your prayers."

5. When he lowers his head, even if not perfectly, reward him and let him know that was correct.

6. Continue this process using the "Say your prayers" cue, but become more selective about how low he bows his head before you reward the behavior, so that he begins to figure out exactly how you want him to do it. When your dog starts to perform it really well, give him extra treats with each perfect or near-perfect completion so he learns to replicate that specific performance.

7. Ultimately, you should be able to give the verbal command while motioning with the treat to get him to complete the trick, and eventually to give the command without motioning.

THE APPLE OF YOUR EYE

Apple picking in a large orchard is one of those activities that really makes you appreciate the season. Check with nearby orchards if they allow dogs before you set out. Keep Leyla on a leash so you can make sure she's not eating fallen apples, which can upset her stomach. Bring the usual supplies, like treats, water and poop bags, and be sure to take advantage of all the space, sights and smells by walking as much of the orchard as you and your dog are up for. At the end of your picking exploits, you might let Leyla sample a bite of the goods or at least give her a dog treat for her exemplary apple-spotting efforts.

MOONWALK

This trick's a "Thriller"!

HOW TO DO IT:

1. If your dog already knows how to back up, this will be a cinch. If not, start by facing your dog with a treat in hand while he's standing, then taking one step toward him, while saying "Back."

2. As soon as he backs up while still facing you, even just a step, reward him with the treat. Continue this process until he can back up a few steps as you approach him while giving the command.

3. If your dog has trouble backing up in a straight line, have him face you with the wall immediately to one side and some type of barricade to the other, so that as you approach him, he'll have to back up straight. Once he's mastered this, remove the barricade and try to perform the trick.

4. When your dog is successful, try giving the "Back" command, but only take one step toward him and use a shooing motion to keep him backing up, if need be. Reward him when he backs away farther from you than you've moved toward him. Eventually, you should be able to say "Back" without having to approach him at all.

5. For a more nuanced "Moonwalk," get your dog to incorporate a crouch that gives his gait a shuffle when he backs up. Reference the Special Forces Crawl trick for how to get your dog lower to the ground, then get him to crouch and shuffle backward with the above steps for how to back up.

BACKYARD WATER PARK

On a hot summer day, give Rex a chance to cool off by frolicking through the sprinklers or making a splash in the kiddy pool. And if he happens to be bath-averse, this can be a more pleasant way to sneak in a little scrub-a-dub-dub!

WHO'S A SHY GUY?

Is Buddy bashful? Show new friends how cute coy can be with this peekaboo trick, whether Buddy is actually timid or really a total ham.

HOW TO DO IT:

1. Have your dog sit in front of you and ask for his paw, if this is a basic trick he has already mastered. If not, skip down to step 4.

2. When he gives you his paw, slowly raise and place it over his eye, asking, "Who's a shy guy?"

3. Give him a treat as soon as he lets you place his paw over his face, and repeat the steps until you can ask, "Who's a shy guy?" and he covers his eyes on his own.

4. If he's having trouble with the trick or doesn't know how to give his paw, have him lie down in front of you and lightly stick a small piece of tape above his eye or his nose so that he can remove it with his paw.

5. When he raises his paw to his face, reward him with praise and a treat. If he fully covers his face, make this reward even more prominent by jackpotting it with extra praise and treats.

6. Once he's gotten good with the tape, remove it and try saying the command while touching his nose or above his eye (wherever you were placing the tape before). When he does, reward him enthusiastically.

7. Finally, when he's mastered it with just the touch, start phasing it out by saying the command, then pointing to his face like you're about to touch it. With repetition, he should eventually do it just by hearing the command.

"Dogs' lives
are too short.
Their only fault,
really."

AGNES SLIGH TURNBULL

BUCKET LIST

10 WAYS YOUR DOG CAN SAVE THE WORLD OR A LIFE!

They saved your life when you rescued them, and now they can make someone else's day brighter. Sometimes it only takes a lick, and sometimes a bit more, but your dog will step up to the challenge, just as you did for him.

- ☐ GREET RETURNING SOLDIERS AT AIRPORTS
- ☐ TRAIN FIDO AS A GUARD DOG
- ☐ BECOME AN EMOTIONAL SUPPORT DOG TO PROVIDE COMFORT TO THOSE IN EMOTIONAL DISTRESS
- ☐ ORGANIZE A DOG WALK FOR CHARITY
- ☐ TRAIN AS A SKI PATROL DOG
- ☐ JOIN A SEARCH AND RESCUE
- ☐ VISIT NURSING HOMES, HOMELESS SHELTERS, AND HOSPITALS TOGETHER
- ☐ TRAIN TO BECOME A WATER RESCUE DOG
- ☐ VISIT COLLEGE CAMPUSES DURING FINAL EXAMS OR MID-TERMS FOR SOME FURRY DE-STRESSING
- ☐ VOLUNTEER AT AN ANIMAL SHELTER TOGETHER

"The better I get to know men, the more I find myself loving dogs."

CHARLES DE GAULLE

BEETHOVEN'S SYMPHONY

If you have a piano or keyboard at home, this trick is a real showstopper; and if you manage to get Lola to play the notes in any harmonic succession, you both deserve a standing ovation.

HOW TO DO IT:

1. Put your keyboard on the floor, or your dog up on a bench where she can safely access the piano or keyboard.

2. Say, "Play the piano," then hold a treat above the keys or place it directly on the keys. Encourage her to jump up on the keys to get the treat. When she does this, reward her enthusiastically.

3. Repeat these steps until you can say, "Play the piano" and have her jump up without having to put the treats down in front of her.

TOUR DE CHAMP

If you enjoy going for bike rides, but feel guilty leaving your pooch behind, a bike trailer, basket or sidecar can be the perfect way to cruise around together, especially if your dog isn't the type who can keep up on foot. Make sure you get acclimated to biking with the dog-toting device over various conditions before Champ takes his inaugural chariot ride. Also be sure to research the safety implications of having your dog in tow before attempting it.

SMOOCHIES!

Lots of dogs will lick your face without needing a command, but those who can give a slobber-free peck on the cheek will seem far more dignified!

 HOW TO DO IT:

1. Get to face level with your dog.

2. Hold a treat to your cheek and say, "Give smoochies."

3. As soon as your dog's nose or muzzle touches your cheek, quickly remove the treat before he can lick you. Then give praise, offering the treat to your dog.

4. Repeat the steps until your dog understands to give you a peck on the cheek on command without holding the treat up. Then try to transfer the trick to others so that your dog will give kisses to them on command as well.

6 WAYS TO GET CREATIVE WITH YOUR POOCH:

1. Hearts and Crafts. Get crafty and create or personalize something for your dog that he or she can use regularly or on special occasions. Even if you've never tried the art form before, Benji will appreciate the ceramic food dish designed, sculpted, and painted by you. Just make sure that the paint can't leach into the food or water and that the dish can be sterilized regularly to prevent bacterial growth. If ceramics aren't your thing, try quilting a blanket or knitting a sweater.

2. Dear Dog Diary. Maybe you're gathering material to write the next *Marley & Me*, or maybe you want a way to remember and treasure all the wonderful moments you'll have with your rescue dog. Whatever your reason for starting a dog journal, it's bound to be something you'll thank your earlier self for taking the time to do each day or week, especially as the years pass and memories fade. A dog journal can also help you track your rescue's progress on behavioral, training or medical issues.

3. Spot's Blogspot. You don't have to be a published author to enjoy creative writing, particularly if it's your dog who has inspired you. Start a novel with Spot in mind, or begin a blog with helpful how-to's or thoughtful opinions from your daily encounters in the dog-o-sphere. You can keep your audience as private or as public as you want—even if your dog is the only member.

4. An Ode to Odie. Whether you play an instrument or just love singing off-key (allegedly), playing or singing to your dog is something you can both enjoy without judgment. If you're really creative, writing a song for your canine object of affection can also be a meaningful (or comical) experience.

5. A Jack (Russell) Pollock Original. Think modern art is so simple a dog could do it? Then put your paint where your paws are and show the Jackson Pollocks of the world how it's done. Place a large poster board or an old sheet on the ground and join your Jack Russell in expressing himself through the medium of nontoxic, washable, animal-safe paint. Just remember to thoroughly wash off *l'artiste* afterward to keep him from cleaning himself off with his tongue. When the artwork is complete, it will brighten a room, as well as your day.

6. Puparazzi Exposure. Whether you have a top-of-the-line Nikon, a smartphone, or a disposable camera you found in the back of your drawer, Fifi will look simply faaaaabulous as the star subject of your doggie photoshoot. Try staging different scenes for holiday cards or snapping some candid shots for a photo contest.

A HOME OF THEIR OWN

Pups that spend time in their yard will appreciate a space all their own to take shelter from the elements, cast shade on a hot day, and serve as a hiding place when the world gets scary. If you're feeling crafty, build your own doghouse with the help of an online tutorial and a nearby home improvement store. Not so great with hammers and nails? The wide world of designer doghouses awaits you online or at most major pet retailers. Just remember that dogs are pack animals who need companionship and socialization, so even if they have a little home of their own, their primary residence should be indoors with you.

THE ROYAL WAVE

It's more than waving "hi"—it's a hello with refinement, style, and something that says, "I'm just a little bit better than you." Teach Mitsy the royal wave, and watch onlookers line up to be her loyal subjects.

HOW TO DO IT:

1. Get your dog to sit in front of you (this is where mastering the simple tricks comes in handy). Hold a treat in your fist and put it up to her within reach. Keep her sitting, and only give her the treat if she taps your fist with her paw. Tap her paw with your free hand if she's having trouble catching on. When she lifts it, make contact with your fist, then give her the treat.

2. Repeat the process until she has caught on that a one-pawed tap to your fist is what you want. Reward her, then put the treat in your other hand, and try getting her to "high-five" your now open hand that once held the treat. Reward her when she high-fives your hand.

3. After she has mastered the high-five, get her to do more of a waving motion by holding your high-five hand slightly out of her reach. Reward her when she lifts her paw and swipes it downward a couple times in a row without actually hitting your hand.

4. Continue this process, but start incorporating a verbal cue before the high-five/wave, like "Wave," "Wave to your subjects," "G'day, Mum," or whatever suits your fancy. Reward each time she completes it successfully, and give extra treats for particularly compelling performances.

5. With enough repetition, you should be able to give your verbal cue without holding up your hand, and your dog will "wave" to all of her loyal subjects.

THE PAW BUMP

Is a queenly gesture a little too stuffy for you and Boomer? Then "pound it out" and "blow it up" like the Obamas on election night!

HOW TO DO IT:

1. Get Boomer to sit down in front of you.

2. Hold a treat out in front of him, just out of reach, making sure he stays seated.

3. When he reaches out for the treat, make contact with your free hand in a fist bumping motion, then give him the treat while making a big fuss.

4. If Boomer takes a while to catch on that you want him to raise his paw, gently tap the back of his leg at the joint to get him to bend his leg. When he does this, reward him with a treat and lots of praise.

5. After he lifts his leg unprompted, gently tap your finger under his paw to get him to raise it higher and reward him.

6. When he gets used to raising his paw to bumping height, say, "Paw bump," and make contact, then give him the treat and lots of praise.

7. Keep repeating these steps until Boomer learns to lift his paw in the bumping motion on command.

TURN ON THE TUBE

Television these days has really gone to the dogs. DIRECTV® offers a 24/7 DOGTV channel scientifically engineered for the senses and interests of canines! Content includes programming for relaxation, stimulation and exposure, ideal for dogs who are left home alone or who experience boredom or anxiety. No TV at home? No worries. DOGTV content can also be streamed online.

PRETTY, PRETTY BALLERINA

It's one thing to say your dog dances, but does he pirouette? This ballerina spinning trick will have the Bolshoi begging him to audition.

 HOW TO DO IT:

1. Have your dog sit in front of you.

2. Hold a treat in front of him and slowly raise it above his head.

3. If your dog stands up on his hind legs, even for a bit, praise him and give him the treat. Depending on how big and what type of dog he is, it may take him a while to get his balance.

4. As your dog is able to stay up on his hind quarters longer, try to get him to spin by saying, "Twirl ballerina!" then holding the treat above his nose and making a slow circular motion with it behind his head. If he turns on his back legs at all, reward him profusely and keep encouraging a full revolution. With enough practice, the verbal command should get him up on his feet faster than you can say "Swan Lake."

NOTE: If you have an older or larger dog, or one with joint issues, this trick may be too difficult or uncomfortable for him. Use your discretion.

"Happiness is
a warm puppy."

CHARLES M. SCHULZ

SPECIAL FORCES CRAWL

Whether it's zero dark thirty or half past noon, little Lucy
can crawl like a commando!

 HOW TO DO IT:

1. Get your dog to lie down.

2. Hold a treat out in front of her nose, close enough to lick, but without letting her grab it.

3. Very slowly begin to drag the treat along the floor.

4. If your dog begins to crawl toward the treat, even just a smidge, get excited
   and give her the treat. However, if she stands up from the crawl position,
   quickly take the treat away and start from the beginning.

5. Repeat these steps, encouraging her to crawl a little bit farther each time
   before giving her the reward.

6. Introduce the verbal cue of "Special Forces Crawl" before signaling to her to begin crawling
   so she begins to understand the verbal cue interchangeably with the original signal.

7. Finally, when she's mastered the crawling, get her to lie down a few yards away from you
   and ask her to perform the Special Forces Crawl all the way to you, jackpotting it when she does.

PIG IN A BLANKET

Hold the cocktail wieners! Your dog will be the life of the party with this Pig in a Blanket trick.

 HOW TO DO IT:

1. This is a trick that combines a few basic tricks, like Lie Down, Take It, and Roll Over. If your dog has already mastered these, you're more than halfway there. If not, remember to take it slow and try not to get frustrated—you'll just wind up frustrating your dog.

2. Place a small blanket on the floor. Get your dog to sit on the blanket first, then motion down with a treat to get her all the way down, using the command "Lie down." Reward her with treats for each increment of progress made in the lying down process, until you get her fully lying and staying down.

3. Once your dog has mastered this, pick up the blanket corner nearest her mouth, shake it a bit, and tell her to "take it," so she puts it in her mouth. As soon as she does this, even for a second, reward her. As you teach this step, start to hold out on rewarding until she holds the blanket corner for a few seconds until you give her the treat.

4. When your dog has gotten good at lying down on the blanket and holding the corner in her mouth, you can then implement the "roll over" command. If your dog doesn't already know how to do this, or if she's anxious about rolling on her back, it may take a while for her to catch on. Be patient and take breaks if the first few tries don't yield any results.

5. To start, get your dog lying down on the blanket, but temporarily skip the "take it" part while teaching "roll over." Once she's lying down, use a treat to motion from in front of her nose in a slow semi-circle rotation toward her tail. This will get her bending to one side. Continue the rotation of the treat while saying "roll over" until she turns onto her back, and at that point, reward the behavior.

6. Continue this process, eventually holding out on the reward until she comes up onto her belly to complete the full "roll over" rotation. Practice this several times, rewarding the behavior until it is progressively what you want it to be.

7. Now that your dog knows "roll over," you can incorporate the roll with the blanket in her mouth. Repeat steps 1 to 4, and while your dog is still holding the blanket in her mouth, give the "roll over" command. If she drops the blanket before rolling, try it again until she understands to keep it in her mouth. This results in her wrapping herself up like a pig in a blanket. Reward even partially correct wrap-ups, and progressively hold out until the full trick is performed.

"If you pick up a starving dog
and make him prosperous
he will not bite you.
This is the principal difference
between a dog and man."

MARK TWAIN

ACHOO!

Gesundheit! Okay, so I really doubt you'll get your dog to say that; however, you can still teach her to bring you a tissue when you sneeze.

 HOW TO DO IT:

1. If your dog is already adept at the sit-stay-release series of commands, that will help you get her to retrieve an object without you throwing it, and without her running off with it.

2. Have your dog sit and stay several yards away from a toy rag on the floor. Give her a verbal cue to go get it and return it to you. Only reward the behavior if she waits for your command to retrieve it and also brings it straight to you without any funny business.

3. Once she has gotten good at retrieval, start putting the rag halfway in a tissue box. Give her the same verbal command to retrieve it out of the box and bring it to you, rewarding only the desired behavior.

4. When she has become comfortable taking the rag out of the box, start incorporating the word "Achoo" before your usual verbal command to retrieve. As you repeat this process, she'll learn that "Achoo" is the trigger, and you can sub out your original retrieval command. Reward her when she starts to get the rag with just "Achoo," but only after she has become successful at retrieving with "Achoo" preceding your original retrieval command.

5. Finally, sub out the rag for the actual tissues in the box. Make sure the first one is prominently sticking out to resemble the rag, and so that it's easy for her to grasp. If she grabs the tissue and doesn't bring it right to you, but instead tears it up or runs away or some other unwanted behavior, don't reward her. Start over until she realizes the reward only comes when she brings the tissue right to you, intact. Then reward her profusely.

There are tons of creative and challenging tricks to teach your dog that can offer as much practical application as amusement. Remember to always keep the experience positive and to take lots of breaks so neither of you get frustrated or lose interest in learning new tricks. Start simple, especially if your dog doesn't already have experience with foundational commands like "sit," "stay," "go get it," etc.

You'll come to see that the process of teaching your dog a trick, no matter how simple, is actually a learning experience for you both. As you're shaping your dog to follow your cues, she's bound to teach you a thing or two about herself that no one else knows, which will draw you even closer together. The payoff of coming to a mutual understanding of a concept, knowing exactly what the other one wants or is likely to do, and executing a synchronized performance will be one of the most rewarding bonding experiences you and your rescue dog will share.

"Here, Gentlemen,
a dog teaches us a
lesson in humanity."

NAPOLEON BONAPARTE

3 TRIP IDEAS FOR YOU AND YOUR POOCH

1. The Housebroken Houseguest

Planning a visit to Aunty Thelma, Cousin Bob, or some old high school buddies? Ask if there's room for one more at the inn, if you know your host won't mind or have an allergy to dogs. If your host has socialized companion animals, the visit can be a good way to acclimate your rescue to new people and animals. Help him build more confidence or teach him to share toys over the course of a weekend, if you feel he's ready for it and your host is on board.

2. Two Tickets to Puppy-dise

Not every vacation necessitates leaving Muttsy with friends or in a kennel. In fact, hotels have increasingly been going animal-friendly, sparing owners and their four-legged companions the separation anxiety in a time that's meant to be carefree. Online travel services like BringFido and Go Pet Friendly can help you locate hotels and campgrounds that permit dogs, as well as provide other helpful information when traveling with your pup.

3. Get Your Licks on Route 66

Many dogs love a good joy ride, as long as the vet or some other unpleasant destination isn't at the end of that road. Turn up the tunes, crack the windows, and enjoy the breeze on your faces. When driving with your dog, make sure he rides only in the back seat and is properly secured with a restraint designed for dogs. Remember to remove the leash once he's secured to ensure it's not closed in the door or stuck on something that can pull him into harm's way. If you're popping into a convenience store, never leave your dog in the car on hot days, when the inside temperature of the car can quickly increase to dangerous levels, even if it's relatively comfortable outside.

BUCKET LIST

15 DOG-FRIENDLY MOVIES TO WATCH WITH YOUR PUP!

Relive your childhood or discover a modern classic with these
pooch-friendly films, all starring dogs! Your pup will love watching these
furry friends tackle their own Bucket-List-Worthy adventures!

- ☐ HOMEWARD BOUND
- ☐ BEETHOVEN
- ☐ THE ADVENTURES OF MILO AND OTIS
- ☐ THE ARTIST
- ☐ A BOY AND HIS DOG
- ☐ BECAUSE OF WINN-DIXIE
- ☐ SHILOH
- ☐ LASSIE
- ☐ BENJI
- ☐ OLD YELLER
- ☐ MARLEY & ME
- ☐ 101 DALMATIANS
- ☐ BEST IN SHOW
- ☐ LADY AND THE TRAMP
- ☐ EIGHT BELOW

HAPPILY EVER AFTER:
REAL-LIFE ADOPTION STORIES

The bond between rescue dogs and their people is best conveyed through the personal stories of those who have experienced it. The following chapter retells the anecdotes of folks from across the country and from all walks of life who have forever been changed for the better by their rescue dog.

Scars & Healing

The Story of Brad & Scarlet
Denville, New Jersey

When Brad met Scarlet, his condition on the inside felt a lot like what the eight-month-old Brittany spaniel looked like on the outside.

Little Scarlet was so shy that it took her a few days to get up the courage to even look at Brad!

"When I got her, she had matted fur and was covered in feces. She was full of infections and parasites, and she couldn't use her back legs very well," he recalls. Scarlet was being kept at a New Jersey shelter that would be shut down for animal cruelty charges and health code violations shortly after Brad adopted her.

He may have rescued Scarlet, but he didn't realize that she would be rescuing him too. After losing his last dog and his fiancée in an ugly breakup, Brad had become very depressed.

Brad was so devoted to helping Scarlet heal that he carried her up and down the stairs for months until she could climb and descend them herself.

"Scarlet came into my life and gave me a purpose," he states. He took Scarlet home and gave her three baths, a haircut, and a good brushing just to get her clean again. But she was so shy from her previous life of neglect that she didn't even venture to look at him for the first couple of days.

"The vets assured me that the infections and sprains in her legs would heal," he says, "I carried her up and down the stairs at my house for the first four months, slowly increasing our walks every week from 20 yards to 50, to 100, and so on," which enabled Scarlet to grow healthier and more confident as time went by.

Scarlet loves helping Brad reel in the big ones on his boat.

Scarlet is now three years old and full of life, leaping into the air in four-foot vertical bounds and zipping up and down the same stairs that Brad had to carry her on for months. The pair is also an avid running, boating and fishing duo.

"She follows me around and is always by my side 24/7," says Brad, "She loves the water and will spend all day swimming and hanging out on the boat." He and Scarlet are often joined by Brad's new long-term girlfriend, Amy, who admits to having fallen in love with both of them.

Though Brad and Scarlet's pain and loneliness are now but distant memories, they haven't forgotten the way they saved each other that day.

"I call her 'Scar' for short," Brad explains, "because she helped me heal the ones you couldn't see."

The days are never long enough for Scarlet, who loves spending them out on the water with her dearest friend.

5 WAYS TO HAVE FUN WITHOUT LEAVING THE HOUSE

1. Staying in for a Walk. In winter weather, or if it's too hot or rainy outside, urban dogs needn't be couch potatoes. If you happen to own a treadmill, this can be a convenient way to go for a walk without going anywhere. Make sure you get your dog acclimated the first few times by keeping the treadmill belt at one slow, steady walking pace before trying more strenuous speeds or durations. However, if she seems anxious or just isn't enjoying herself, give her the chance to opt out.

2. Elevate Your Workout. If you don't have the luxury of a treadmill at your disposal, climbing and descending stairwells in a multifamily building is another great indoor activity for both dogs and humans, as long as joint problems are not an issue for either of you.

3. Get Stoked. When the weather outside is frightful, it can be the perfect time to curl up beside the fireplace with a book and your best friend. Put on a relaxing playlist or get playful and roast S'mores (chocolate-free for Smokey). However you choose to bask in the glow, you probably won't get many complaints from your dog.

4. Flicks with Trixie. Hunker down in front of the tube with a big bowl of popcorn and your fur-ever friend for a movie night of inspirational dog flicks. *Best in Show, Turner & Hooch, Beethoven, Marley & Me, Homeward Bound,* and *The Adventures of Milo and Otis,* are just a few of the many recent favorites, not to mention oldies-but-goodies like *Lassie* and *Old Yeller,* or animated features like *Lady and the Tramp* and *All Dogs Go to Heaven.*

5. Raise the Flag at Fort McFurry. Remember building blanket forts as a kid? Whether you have kids of your own now, or it's just you and the pooch, reliving this childhood indoor activity will be beloved by all. According to the American Humane Association, dogs are den animals that like having small, enclosed places to go to feel secure. So pull the pillows off the couch and the linens off the bed; it's time to build a den for your wolf pack.

One Adoption
that Led to 2,000

The Story of Jacqueline & Blake
Bloomingdale, New Jersey

It was 2002, and the American craze for oodles of Doodles began taking the nation by storm. The spike in demand for designer dog breeds, like the Labradoodle, quickly caused an influx of puppies to be bred. For some who purchased these dogs, the realities of being a caregiver was more than they were prepared for, and many puppies and adult Labradoodles wound up in shelters.

On his first day home with Jacqueline, Blake was suffering from mange and was shaved down to the skin.

In August of 2007, Jacqueline headed to a shelter in search of her own dog. She had recently been through a difficult break-up, and was feeling frustrated and unfulfilled at her job. At the shelter, she encountered a six-month-old cream-colored Labradoodle with pale green eyes and a pink nose. The dog was underweight and, by the smell of him, in desperate need of a bath.

"He had mange, parvo, and every worm under the sun," recalls Jacqueline; but that didn't stop the puppy from coming right up to her, tail wagging, to lick her arm and lay his head on her shoulder as she crouched down beside him.

"He picked me," she says softly, a smile forming across her face.

Jacqueline got the puppy home and decided on the name Blake, though she'll be the first to tell you she calls him a dozen other affectionate nicknames—Budge, Butterbean, Buddha, Fluffernutter, Sy Noodleman (his Hebrew name), and Blakey Blakey Eggs and Bakey, to name just a few.

Blake with a snoot full of snow, loving his own winter wonderland.

Blake appeared to have never stepped on grass before, based on his perplexed reaction to the yard. It would also be a hard-fought few weeks to get him healthy. The mange flared up, and the parvovirus caused him to vomit and pass bloody diarrhea for days, leaving him in agony. With steady I.V. fluids, medication, dewormers, and meticulous care, Jacqueline and veterinarians were eventually able to restore Blake's health. After two months, his hair had even grown in enough to look like a true Doodle.

Jacqueline was absolutely in love—but growing in her was a desire to help other Doodles headed toward fates similar to Blake's before she'd found him. Within less than a year of adopting Blake, she started her own tiny rescue operation out of her one-bedroom apartment, locating Doodles who needed good homes and matching them with qualified adopters.

Her organization would not stay tiny for long. Jacqueline credits the rapid growth of her Doodle Rescue Collective (DRC) to the swiftly burgeoning influence of social media sites, like Facebook. "All of a sudden, it was much easier for me to rescue Doodles and talk about them on Doodle-specific media sites and get them placed into great homes," she says. The DRC was also one of the first rescues to use social media to place dogs, recruit volunteers, and fundraise.

Just months after founding the organization, Jacqueline filed for 501c3 (nonprofit) status and was approved. To date, the DRC has facilitated more than 2,000 adoptions across North America, with the help of 1,000 registered volunteers.

Jacqueline went on to adopt and foster several more Doodles, four of which still live with her today. Blake, Bella, Sully and Daisy keep "Casa del Doodle," as she refers to her home, full of comical shenanigans and, of course, love.

Reflecting back on that August day, Jacqueline is amazed by how her passion blossomed into a successful and purposeful career. What's more, her search for her soulmate concluded with four paws and an unconditional bond.

"Blake saved my life," she muses, "I didn't save him."

Jacqueline and Blake are an inseparable duo.

4 IDEAS FOR GOOD CLEAN FUN

I Feel Pretty, Oh So Pretty! If you've done your research, and you're up to the challenge, grooming your dog yourself can be a great bonding experience—though it will definitely be a learning experience, for starters. Check out some helpful grooming pointers from the ASPCA, located in the Resources section, before you get started.

Rub-a-Dub-Dub, Tips for the Tub. Though you may approach bathing your dog with great zeal, the likelihood is that she will not. Since bathing is a necessary evil (necessary to you, evil to her), try to associate it with things your dog enjoys, like treats, belly rubs, a fun game, etc. Also be sure to go slowly and gently in both the acclimation process and the actual bathing.

The Perfect Paw-dicure. Make the nail-trimming regimen enjoyable for both of you by purchasing the proper tools, learning the right techniques, and fostering a quiet, stress-free environment with treats offered at the end. Slow, steady and soothing should be your mantra, like you're giving Lady the royal nail salon spa treatment.

The Next Crest® Kid. Okay, so executing good dental hygiene may not be the epitome of a fun time, but it is an important activity for you and your dog to do together—separate brushes, of course. The ASPCA recommends brushing your dog's teeth daily or at least a few times a week to prevent periodontal disease. Use dog-specific paste, trying out which flavor your dog likes best. Remember to take it slow, if this is a new phenomenon for your rescue hound. You may want to first acclimate her to having her muzzle handled before introducing a toothbrush and paste. Then be sure to associate positive things with tooth brushing to keep her from becoming anxious by the experience.

"The dog has been esteemed and loved by all the people on earth and he has deserved this affection for he renders services that have made him man's best friend."

ALFRED BARBOU

Sweet as Honey

The Story of Dane & Honey
Savannah, Georgia

It was a charitable act that turned into a bond for life. In June of 2013, a Labradoodle puppy named Honey caught Dane's attention in a video on the Doodle Rescue Collective's (DRC) Facebook page.

Honey's previous owner had purchased her from a puppy mill, and by four months of age, it became clear that Honey had serious problems. Most noticeably, says Dane, "she couldn't stand up on her own, because her back knees were deformed," likely due to generations of inbreeding. Honey was also riddled with intestinal diseases that caused her to have trouble holding her bowels.

When Honey wound up with the DRC, she was about seven or eight months old. The rescue transported her from Seattle, Washington, to the home of Sheri and Mike, her foster parents in Cincinnati, Ohio.

A MAZE OF MAIZE

When a dog's nose and a person's sense of direction (or lack thereof) square off in a maze race, which will find their way out the other side first? That's an entertaining question to answer in a corn maze. Try running through first without Goober and timing your attempt, then see how long it takes him to find the person calling him from the other side. If he's reluctant to leave you, conquer the maze together and see if he remembers the right turns to make on your second time through. Keep in mind, Goober might improvise and create his own "short cut!"

"They did an awesome job at giving her the love and confidence she needed," says Dane.

But their vet realized that Honey would need a sophisticated double knee replacement, requiring her to be transported yet again, this time to Alvarado, Texas, for surgery. Hearing this, Dane

Honey buckled up and ready to go to her new "forever" home.

offered to drive to Cincinnati from his home in Savannah, Georgia, to pick her up and take her the 36 hours to Alvarado. And so they set off together to cross a large stretch of the country.

"By that time, we had been together about 33 hours, and I had fallen in love with her," he recalls. Honey had quickly become attached as well, snuggling up to him at the motel and snoring through the night.

The orthopedic surgeon explained it would take until July for Honey to recover enough to be released. Aware that he'd have to leave her for several weeks, Dane crawled up to Honey, nose-to-nose, and whispered a promise: "I'll be back for you." He then headed home to Savannah.

Dane kept his promise; on July 16, he returned to Alvarado. The vet staff was waiting under a tree with Honey and a video camera when he arrived. Honey beamed at him with her "signature smile."

"She came up to me and just smothered me with kisses," Dane says joyfully. All the way home, she hugged the "Froggy Face" pillow Dane had given her on their way down to Texas.

Honey and her brothers Guinness (middle) and Rosco (far left) posing for their photo op at the Mayport Navy Base RV park in Jacksonville, Florida.

"It was just a beautiful drive all the way back," he muses.

Honey met Dane's wife, Joyce, and their two other Doodles, Roscoe and Guinness, and the whole O'Doodle clan immediately became inseparable. They helped Honey strengthen her legs by swimming at the beach and walking regularly. Joyce would often groom Honey, who is now 70 pounds—the largest of the three dogs. Then, every night, Honey would fall asleep on Joyce's lap.

Honey comforting her ill Mommy.

When the family took in a foster puppy who had been on the streets most of his life, "Honey took to him right away," says Dane, "It's almost like she mothered him. He learned what not to do, and what he could do." Within three months, the puppy was well behaved, and a forever family adopted him. Honey also became very close to a 12-year-old foster that Dane took in from a shelter, where dogs were routinely euthanized for space constrictions. The dog had been abandoned there by his family of many years, but after Honey's nurturing, he too went on to be adopted.

When Joyce fell ill with pancreatitis in 2014, Honey became her devout nursemaid. Then, in 2015, Joyce was diagnosed with pancreatic cancer. Honey, Roscoe and Guinness became very anxious, knowing intuitively that something was wrong. Joyce passed away six weeks later, with all three dogs pressed tightly to her side.

Life without Joyce was hard to accept for Dane and the dogs, though they move forward in her memory every day. The foursome continues to travel often, encountering wildlife and sea creatures wherever they go.

"Roscoe and Guinness have swam in the Gulf, the Atlantic, all five Great Lakes, the Mississippi River, and countless ponds, lakes and rivers in between," says Dane, "They've been to the Grand Canyon, Death Valley, and near the top of Mt. McKinley—you name it." Though Honey isn't as well traveled yet as her brothers, she absolutely loves adventure and makes excellent use of her senses.

Back at home, she enjoys chasing the neighbors' trucks, ATVs, and motorcycles up and down Dane's 200-foot fence line. When she's all tuckered out, she can be found "vegging out on the couch" with her head in Dane's lap.

On New Years' Eve, Honey's former foster parents, Sheri and Mike, come to visit from Cincinnati. Needless to say, the wobbly puppy has come much farther than anyone could have guessed, thanks to the loving people who got her on her feet.

FRANKENPOOCH MEETS COUNT DOGULA

Who isn't a sucker for a pug dressed like a giant tarantula, or a dachshund wedged into a hot dog bun costume? As long as your pooch is safe and comfortable in his or her outfit, Halloween and other costumed events can be tons of fun (and probably worth a good chuckle) for you and Princess Pooch.

"Dogs are not our whole life, but they make our lives whole."

ROGER A. CARAS

Stealing the Spotlight

The Story of Casey, Staci & Spottie
Austin, Texas

It may sound like an unusual way to adopt a dog, but then again, Austin, Texas, prides itself on being an unusual place. Staci and her husband Casey met Spottie several years ago, when an insurance agency was giving away puppies.

"I couldn't pass up all of those spots!" exclaims Staci, who named the dog after them. "Spottie Ann" even shares the same initials as Staci.

"I wasn't sure what Spottie would think of city life, but, as my mom said, 'She's happy when she's with y'all, wherever that may be.'"

Spots and Stripes: Spottie manages the household while Staci and Casey are at work.

Spottie is now eight and loving life with Staci and Casey.

"We take her everywhere we go," says Casey, "Her most favorite thing is 'going' somewhere—anywhere! Even if it's a simple trip to town. She rides on the center console of the truck, and I call her my 'Road Dawg.'"

"Another favorite is to be 'looking' for anything moving outside," he adds, "She will run, slide, and let out a threatening or territorial bark. Spottie is small, but acts as though she rules the roost. She gives kind growls to the other family hounds so they know who is boss!"

Spottie vigilantly spotting for any sign of trespassing people or critters.

Casey and Spottie getting in a snuggle or two.

Besides being the Big Kahuna, Spottie has the very important job of managing Staci and Casey's household while they're away at work during the day. When the couple returns, Spottie wedges herself right between the two to catch up on all the cuddling she missed while they were out.

"She is the best cuddler!" Staci gushes, "The closer the better, in her book."

Spottie is also a non-discriminatory food enthusiast, intent on licking every last fleck of edible matter from humans' dinner plates. "Breffast" is a beloved Spottie mealtime.

"When we're at my parents' house, each dog gets a fried egg on the weekend," says Staci, "In the evenings, when it's bedtime, they all must be at attention sitting on their beds, and then my dad either tosses them popcorn or their usual Milk-Bone."

"There is never a dull moment with Spottie," says Staci, "We can't express the joy she brings to our life. I truly think that God made dogs to help us see what unconditional love really is. Every human could learn a lesson from Man's Best Friend."

Staci and Spottie digging post holes by hand at Staci's parents' cabin.

"Dogs provide us with
a never-ending supply
of presents."

ROBB PEARLMAN

The Girl from Sayulita

The Story of Chris & Chata
Portland, Oregon

Tall and tan and young and lovely" … well, not quite. This girl wasn't from Ipanema, and if Sinatra had sung about her, it probably would have gone more like, "Brindle and drooling and hungry and dirty."

Chris was on vacation, surfing with friends in Sayulita, Mexico, in December 2013. It's a city where stray dogs can be seen foraging for food in the streets day and night. Chris says he "really didn't think anything of it," until the second day of his trip. As he walked out of the ocean, he noticed one of his friends—a retired firefighter they called "The Big Angry"—bickering with a stray Boxer, who had approached him curiously as he sat on the sand.

Chata in Chris's shop.

"The dog was drooling and stunk," recalls Chris, "She looked like she had a bad leg and a missing eye."

In spite of her downtrodden appearance and The Big Angry's evident frustration (which might be expected given his nickname), "I almost immediately liked the dog," says Chris, "Number one, it was hilarious to listen to the interaction between her and Big Angry, and the dog was such a debacle that she was actually pretty cute."

Chris took the dog back to the house where they were staying, cleaned her eye, gave her some food, and let her sleep in the courtyard.

Chata rockin' out to some tunes.

"The next morning, we went to drive to a different beach, but the dog started chasing the car!

"I was afraid she would get hurt, so I took her into a shop and asked if the owner would hold her while I drove off," Chris explains.The shop owner knew the dog by name: Chata. "Now we're getting somewhere," Chris thought to himself. "When I got back home that evening, the dog was sitting in front of the gate to my house, waiting."

Chata got another good meal, a bed, and some more much-needed cleaning. The next day, the same chase scene played out with the shop owner having to hold Chata back from running after the car.

"I decided that if the dog was there again that afternoon, I would think about adopting her," says Chris. When he returned, he was delighted to find her waiting.

The following day was Chris's last in town, and he had to catch a bus back to Puerto Vallarta to fly home to Portland, Oregon.

"I spent the morning at the Sayulita shelter, where they informed me of Chata's checkered past of abuse, adoption, breeding and abandonment," he says, "The shelter had me convinced that immigration and rescue was the best option."

Chris spent the rest of the morning running to vets in Mexico to get Chata immunizations and quarantine paperwork before buying her a plane ticket to Los Angeles. His friend, Whitney, had to fly Chata, since Chris's airline would not allow her aboard.

"Once we got back to Portland, I introduced Chata to her new family: Belli Dog and my son Oscar. It has been two years, and her English is getting better," says Chris, as though Chata were a Mexican foreign exchange student. Chata is house-trained and gets along well with everyone.

"We often refer to her as Zuul, the character from Ghostbusters, because of the sounds she makes, along with the drool," Chris jokes. Chata, nevertheless, is happy, healthy … and appears to be unoffended by the comparison.

"I don't regret taking her from her beach home at all," reflects Chris, "but I do hope to take her back for a visit at some point."

BARK AVENUE

Everyone loves a good shopping spree, and when stores open their doors to dogs, it's clear that humans aren't alone in their enjoyment. Besides stores with inventory for companion animals, there is an ever-increasing number of human stores that will allow Duchess to make her debut. So grab your leash and a credit card; there are shoes to be bought for future chewing!

BUCKET LIST

FIVE WAYS TO PAMPER YOUR POOCH

Being a faithful companion is hard work.
Here are some ways to show your pup that you care.

- ☐ TAKE FIDO TO A MASSEUSE,
  OR MASSAGE HIM YOURSELF

- ☐ TAKE A NAP TOGETHER IN THE SUNSHINE

- ☐ MAKE HOMEMADE DOG-FRIENDLY POPSICLES
  (USING COCONUT MILK!) TO SHARE

- ☐ PURCHASE DOG-SAFE SHAMPOO AND GIVE
  YOUR PUP A BUBBLE BATH

- ☐ SIGN UP FOR BARKBOX AND ENJOY MONTHLY TREATS

3 ACTIVITIES FOR WINTER FUN

It's Showtime for Snow Time! Many dogs love playing in the snow, if it's at a manageable height for them, and the temperature and conditions aren't dangerously harsh. If you plan on venturing out, look into recommended cold-weather gear for your type of canine to ensure his or her core and extremities are adequately protected for the conditions.

Head for the Hills. You don't have to be a kid to get excited for sledding, and Rex is bound to share your excitement. Have him ride in your lap, or let him give chase as you careen down the snow-covered hillside. Just make sure that the area is either fenced in or that Rex is a pro at coming back when called, even with lots of distractions, and especially if the sledding hill is near a road.

Snowball Fight! What's a snowfall without a good snowball fight? You may be on the winning end of this battle, but we have a feeling your dog will love every snowball that comes her way. Duck behind trees and snowbanks and let her chase you down. Toss snowballs up in the air for her to catch, and watch her delight (and maybe surprise) when she catches a snoot full of snow!

Her Friend, Her Keeper

The Story of Katie & Keeper
Covington, Louisiana

T here's no saying what set it off or why, and at this point, it may not even matter. What's certain, though, is the car is where it started, and where it would come full circle.

It was 2010, and Katie was in bad shape. Her first panic attack had happened earlier that year while driving her car, causing her emotional state to take a precipitous downturn. Katie's anxiety disorder eventually got so bad that, by the following year, she couldn't even bring herself to leave the house. She began to miss class after class at law school, and she was nowhere to be found at social outings. Even routine tasks like grocery shopping became insurmountable.

Keeper during his first days home with Katie.

"My mom had to come live with me for a month just to help me walk out the door to the mailbox," Katie recalls. Most terrifying of all to her was the idea of getting back in a car.

Katie's doctor at the time suggested that she get a dog—another living creature to care for besides herself, which could serve as a distraction, a comfort, and a purpose to wake up in the morning. The doctor located a dog in the process of earning his therapy dog certification and put Katie in touch with the rescue.

GOOD DOGS GONE NAUTI-CAL

Whether it's a lake, a river, or the great blue sea, and you're floating in a dinghy, a sailboat, or hundred-foot yacht, bring Bowser along on your nautical quest, wherever it may take you. Even if they're not the type to jump in the water, many dogs appreciate a cruise. Just remember that the sun is extra bright reflecting off the water, and even strong swimmers can get in over their heads. Equipment like doggy sunglasses, sunblock, and life preservers are therefore highly encouraged.

Katie's favorite co-pilot.

"From the moment I met him, he was a keeper," she says. In fact, the dog was such a keeper, Katie made it his namesake and adopted him on the spot.

"The most important part about Keeper is that he loves the car," explains Katie, which was an instrumental factor in getting her back into one. In fact, Keeper gets so excited for car rides, Katie and her husband Court encourage him to run laps around the backyard to tucker him out before he hops in.

When Keeper isn't riding in cars, he's a bit of a gourmand. "He actually sleeps with his head on the food bowl," Katie admits, "He's been on a diet—twice—to no avail."

"Keeper's favorite thing to do, besides eat and ride in the car, is to lay on the couch and cuddle," she adds, "He'd lay with you in a hospital bed until they made him leave."

Though Keeper is a triumphant eater and has attained the highest belt possible in couch potato ju-jitsu, it might come as a surprise that this prolific pup is also a local celebrity at the dog park.

Keeper and his sister Cody get decked out in costumes for Halloween.

"We never see Keeper once we walk through the gate, because he spends the entire time socializing," declares Katie, "He just goes from group to group, from dog to dog, sniffing butts, getting pet, and being cooed at. The only exercise he gets is trotting after dogs he hasn't said 'hi' to yet."

Katie and Court joke that Keeper's dream job would be a dog food deliveryman. "Then he could combine all of his favorites: riding in the car to deliver kibble and socializing," she laughs, "If not that, maybe a Walmart greeter."

The whole family posing for their annual holiday card photo.
(From left to right: Katie, Yams, Cody, Court, and Keeper.)

BACKYARD STARGAZERS

If you can't make it to a remote campground, but you have a yard, you and Shadow can still lie under the stars and let the crickets' lullaby sing you to sleep. On a clear evening, pitch a tent with plenty of blankets, a flashlight, and whatever else you may need, and spend the night outdoors with your pack mate, the way the earliest humans and canines did.

All in the Family

The Story of Ashley & Coco
and Jayson & Bucky
Fresno, California

A shley decided she wanted to adopt a dog in 2011.

"I always knew the only way I would get a dog would be by rescuing one, since there are so many that are in need of homes," she explains.

While visiting Central Valley Animal Lovers (CVAL), Ashley kept noticing a soft, brown dog that "looked like cocoa" out of the corner of her eye. "Actually, I probably noticed her because she was so hyper!" she jokes, "She had this adorable puppy face!"

Ashley and Coco enjoy a snuggle and a selfie.

Ashley didn't want a puppy, but fortunately for Coco, even though she looked like a puppy, she wasn't. While she was talking to one of the CVAL staff, Coco climbed the x-pen she was in and jumped right into Ashley's arms! Four years later, Coco still has a puppy face, though she has calmed down a bit.

"She's my best friend, and getting her was one of the best decisions I've ever made!" Ashley exclaims.

CLOCK IN WITH CLEO

If you're lucky enough to work for an organization that observes Take Your Dog to Work Day® (or you're able to convince them for the first time this year), consider capitalizing on the opportunity, if your dog is well-behaved and won't stress in the new atmosphere (which even us humans can have trouble with—it is work, after all!) Various studies indicate that having your dog at work can reduce stress and even increase productivity, collaboration and morale, among other benefits.

The day Bucky joined the family.

A year after adopting Coco, Ashley began dating Jayson, and the pair adopted another dog named Bucky.

"Bucky is a very simple dog, loyal and loving. His presence brings a calmness with it," says Ashley. Bucky is an avid lounger, snuggler and kiss-giver. He also loves to snooze.

"When he sleeps, he groans like an old man, and it's pretty funny," laughs Ashley, "We always say, 'Oh, sorry, are we being too loud, Bucky?'"

Though Jayson wanted to make Bucky a hunting dog, he and Ashley quickly learned that that plan just wasn't in the cards.

"Bucky is a big scaredy-cat," explains Ashley. He gets extremely frightened by gun shots and fireworks. And water. Needless to say, Bucky is not a fan of hunting or swimming. However, he's not the only one in the house with a phobia. His sister Coco is terrified of … laundry! (After weeks of ignoring our own hampers, Coco, we know how you feel.)

"Whenever I fold laundry, she runs and hides under the bed," says Ashley. Under the bed is Coco's personal hiding spot, where she also hides other things, besides her own scaredy rump.

When Coco and Bucky aren't quaking in their collars, they take great joy in many activities. Coco and Ashley play games, especially during mealtimes. "I'll ask her to 'pay me the money,' and she'll give me her paw, and I'll give her a treat—usually some of whatever I'm eating," says Ashley.

Bucky learned to shake hands, just by watching Coco. "He'll just walk up to you and throw his paw at you like, 'Hey, I'm shaking. Do I get something now?'"

Another Coco-ism Bucky picked up is when they're in front of the tube. If there are any animals on TV, they bark and run up to the screen and get up on their hind legs. Maybe they're just making sure no other animals horn in on their time with Ashley and Jayson.

Coco with her beloved pink squeaky chicken.

"When I get home from being around other animals, Bucky interrogates me by smelling the same spot obsessively," says Ashley. As for Coco, "She should have been named Shadow, because she follows me everywhere I go," she says, "If I go into the bathroom and close the door, she whines outside. She brings me a toy every time I walk in the door, and she's beside herself with excitement."

Coco *loves* toys, her favorites being her pink and yellow squeaky chickens. She also has a monkey. If asked to bring one back by name, she knows exactly which is which. You can tell Coco is happy when she smiles and her eyes get all squinty, says Ashley.

"Jayson considers Bucky his dog and Coco my dog, but really they're both our dogs," Ashley remarks thoughtfully, "We all wouldn't be complete without each other. We are all a family."

The Runt Who Wouldn't Hunt

The Story of Lori and Lilly
Springfield, Missouri

Lilly is a special soul—there's no doubt about it.

Born on an 11,000-acre ranch resort outside of Fort Worth, Texas, she and all of her littermates had been bred to hunt and accompany ranch guests on hunting excursions. But it was clear from the start that Lilly would never be like the others.

As the runt of the litter, one of the hunting guides took her under his wing just to keep her alive, feeding her milk through an eyedropper, week after week. As Lilly grew stronger, the hunting guide tried to train her to hunt upland birds and, as it so happened, she had a great nose for pointing.

Lilly while living on the Texas hunting ranch.

SHARING THE JOY

Plenty of people who love animals are not able to own them or may seldom even get to see them. This is especially true for folks living in long-term care facilities. Fortunately, many of these places allow dogs to visit for therapeutic purposes, provided they have a particular designation or certification. If you and your pup have the desire to brighten an ill, disabled or elderly person's day, check with your local healthcare facility about their therapy dog visitation requirements.

Lori, Lilly and Henry love to go exploring.

But Lilly was a free spirit who marched to the beat of her own drummer. Instead of retrieving the fallen birds for the hunters, who paid for the experience, she would run away with the bird in her mouth to give it a proper burial. When it became clear that gentle Lilly was not made for a life of hunting, she was no longer welcome at the ranch. The hunting guide relinquished her to his colleague Lori shortly after she had lost her Blue Heeler.

"Lilly has always had the kindest, softest spirit and a healing love," says Lori, "She's traveled all over the nation with me, bringing her beautiful smile and quiet kindness to all she encounters. She's even been featured in a bridal spread in *Indulge* magazine, because of her gentle, loving nature."

In addition to being a one-time fashion model, Lilly is also a model citizen. She and Lori often volunteer at long-term care facilities, visiting and comforting those who may be feeling despondent, immobile and alone.

"Lilly has always brought the sweetest smiles to the people we find there," says Lori, "She's always been so gentle and heals those who are hurting."

Lilly and Lori, best buds for life.

When Lilly isn't busy brightening someone else's day, she's the highlight of Lori's. The two enjoy boating, road trips, and hanging out on the couch to watch Netflix marathons.

Lori and Lilly have spent nearly 10 years together now, many filled with joy, and some punctuated by personal challenges. Through a couple of romantic disappointments and a long, lonely job relocation to a remote part of the country, Lori had Lilly to help her through the rough patches.

"Dogs are one of life's greatest teachers, without having to say a word," says Lori. Lilly has been a major support system in her life. Today, however, it is Lilly who will need the support, whether she is aware of it yet or not.

Lilly was recently diagnosed with mammary cancer. Lori has started Lilly on a treatment regimen and is trying all options possible. In the meantime, she says, Lilly does not seem to notice anything is different; she is still the same sweet girl with the heartwarming disposition and lovable Lilly smile. Together, those smiles will help them through the hard-fought battle to come for the gentle runt who refused to hunt.

MAKE LIKE A TREE (AND LEAVES!)

Your hard work of raking leaves is finally done (or maybe a landscaper did it for you), and Scruffy is just squirming to get out there and tear into that big pile of red, gold and crunchy brown. The good news is, if he's equipped with flea and tick repellant, he's pretty much safe to have at it, as long as no sharp or dangerous things are lurking in the pile. The bad news? Scruffy can't operate the rake when the fun is done.

Heroes on the Front Lines

The Story of Mardu, Ron
and their Troop
Moorpark, California

On any given day, it's "reigning" cats and dogs at the southern California home of Mardu and her husband Ron, where their five dogs and three cats rule the roost. The couple got involved volunteering in the rescue community back in 1997, with an initial focus on helping cats; but it wasn't long before Ron began longing for a dog to join their household. His rescue of a golden retriever named Goldie would set in motion a series of fosters and adoptions that would change Ron and Mardu's lives permanently.

Dexter the Maltipoo looked like a whole new dog after Mardu rescued him.

"Goldie was probably the ugliest golden retriever I'd ever seen," admits Mardu, explaining the severity of the dog's skin conditions that kept half her body shaved. But where love grows, so can practically anything. With Mardu and Ron's impeccable care, "all of her hair eventually came back, and she was absolutely stunning," Mardu recalls.

When Goldie passed away from cancer six years later, the couple's grief brought them to rescue a Wheaton Terrier mix named Quincy, with whom they enjoyed five or six wonderful years before he passed away from a stroke.

"It just became a collection [of animals] afterward," says Mardu, referencing the three cats and five dogs, all of whom she and Ron rescued over the years. The eight animals get along very well, like a real world Brady Bunch family.

First there was Bentley the Golden doodle, who Mardu and Ron adopted through the Doodle Rescue Collective. Then there was Dexter, the Maltipoo Mardu found at a rescue in Newbury Park, California.

Stempel made a surprise entrance into Mardu and Ron's life on the day they said goodbye to Ron's mother, who Stempel is named after.

"He was in such bad shape, you couldn't see through the mats," she remembers, "Everybody was looking at the Puggle next to him, but no one was looking at Dexter." Fortunately for the tangled brown mass, Mardu only had eyes for him. The rescue staff took Dexter for a buzz and a scrub that, when he emerged, left a white "froufrou" dog standing in his place. Mardu could hardly believe it was the same animal, but resolved to bring him to Ron.

"I didn't ask for permission; I asked for forgiveness, and took him home," she says. To this day, Dexter will hardly leave her side.

Stempel, the Chihuahua-Dachshund mix, found his way into the couple's car and hearts on the same day they buried Ron's mother. The dog was a stray running through the California farmlands with no chip or tags. Mardu had to jam on the breaks to avoid hitting him—he then jumped into their car as if he'd been waiting for his ride. Tried as they might to find his owner, Stempel was never claimed, which is why he now carries Ron's mother's maiden name.

"I kind of felt like he was a little gift from her," Mardu muses, recalling Stempel's impeccable timing and an uncanny conversation with her mother-in-law about a Chihuahua shortly before her passing.

Dopey the foster dog became a permanent member of Mardu and Ron's troop.

Stempel, Dexter and Bentley live with Tucker the Cockapoo and Dopey the white Chihuahua, who Mardu affectionately calls their "foster fail," since he was supposed to be placed in a forever home that happily became their own.

"There's no greater gratification than fostering and seeing them go through all those stages of transformation," explains Mardu. All the dogs are highly socialized, and they go to work with Ron every day, enjoying free rein of the office.

When Ron and Mardu aren't running a business, they're on the front lines of the animal rescue and Veterans Affairs communities, expertly pairing animals in need of a home with veterans in need of emotional support or companionship. Mardu and Ron started their own Pets for Vets chapter in Ventura County, California, on May 1, 2014. The program serves veterans with traumatic brain injuries, anxiety, depression, Post-Traumatic Stress Disorder, and a variety of other circumstances that merit therapy animals. Mardu and Ron are flooded with local veteran referrals and requests. They now also have two Vietnam vets on staff as professional dog trainers, who assess veteran and dog candidates for the best potential matches. The process is slow and methodical; "It's about the quality of the match, not the quantity," explains Mardu. The trainer first works exclusively with the veteran to understand his or her needs, lifestyle, and stress triggers.
These factors are key influencers of which dog, cat, or even bird the trainer selects from local shelters, as are the animal's temperament, behavior, and energy level. Emotional Support Dogs (ESD) may need to wake veterans up from night terrors, distract them from panic attacks, or perform a 360-degree clearance around their owner in public to prevent people from startling them. It's not until a trainer is practically certain that a match will work out that the animal is introduced to the intended veteran. Mardu and Ron's own troop helps promote their cause by sporting Pets for Vets t-shirts and demonstrating what ESD do.

"They're really a great example of the program," she remarks. And like the servicemen and women whom their work benefits, they're also each other's adopted family.

BUCKET LIST

'TIS THE SEASON TO CELEBRATE WITH YOUR DOGGY!

Make Fido part of the festivities this season, and spread holiday cheer
all year long! Your pup can have a blast with you joining in on
all the family and friends fun.

- ☐ HOST AN "EASTER EGG HUNT"
  (WITH DOG TREATS) FOR FIDO AND HIS FRIENDS

- ☐ HANG STOCKINGS FOR YOUR RESCUE(S)
  OVER THE MANTLE AT CHRISTMAS

- ☐ RAKE A PILE OF LEAVES AND LEAP RIGHT INTO IT TO
  CELEBRATE FALL!

- ☐ SHARE TURKEY (OR TOFURKY®!) AT THANKSGIVING
  (BUT NO TURKEY BONES!)

- ☐ WEAR MATCHING HALLOWEEN COSTUMES

Into the Mystic

The Story of Max & Morrison
Louisville, Colorado

Morrison the Golden Retriever did not get the best start at life. Confined as a stud dog on a puppy mill somewhere in Missouri, his role there was not as easy as one might guess. When local police entered the facility on a child abuse investigation in 2010, they found several dogs in deplorable condition, including Morrison.

Morrison, happy and healthy long after his rescue from a puppy mill.

"From what we could tell, it was likely that he had never been out of his cage, because he didn't know how to run," recalls Max. Morrison was also riddled with worms, which nearly took his life within the first week that Max and his wife adopted him. Had the police not confiscated the dogs when they did, it could have been curtains for poor (Van) Morrison (Max's ex-wife's favorite musician), not to be confused with Jim Morrison, who made an early exit himself.

Now long since "The Healing has Begun," Morrison is a healthy, happy eight-year-old, who is more active than he could have ever dreamed of from his cage at the puppy mill. Though Max and his wife have since separated, their continued friendship enables Max to spend a lot of time with Morrison.

Max, Dakota, and Morrison on a snowshoe adventure.

"We like to hike together," says Max, "He loves to be out on the trail exploring." They're always accompanied by the "Brown-eyed Girl," Dakota, Max's yellow Labrador.

Morrison and sister Dakota are always up for a swim.

Another one of Morrison's favorites is snowshoeing. He and Max enjoy the Colorado winters by trekking "Into the Mystic" on long excursions. He even has his own state-of-the-art snow boots, just like Max! When he isn't in full gear, Morrison still adores the snow and every way to play in it. In the summer months, he's busy swimming and retrieving, understanding better than most that "You Don't Push the River."

"I take him to the reservoir here to swim," says Max, "He's not the fastest swimmer, but he does a great job." Max adds that, even as Morrison gets older, he "hasn't showed any signs of slowing."

And that energy is important when the three amigos head for the "Bright Side of the Road" to go four-wheeling in Max's Jeep. "I strap them both in with a harness and seat belt," Max explains, "Morrison loves being close to his people, and he's always by my side."

Both pooches are pooped after an active day of four-wheeling in Max's Jeep.

"I'd say what makes our relationship special is that we have each other's back," says Max, "Morrison is such a good therapy dog that, when I've had a tough day, he always knows it. In return, I keep him safe, feed him, and take him on adventures."

It's the deal of a lifetime for the dog and the man who happened to find each other, and who have a profound appreciation for the simple things in life, particularly "Days Like This."

"Dogs laugh,
but they laugh
with their tails."

MAX EASTMAN

Third Chance Is a Charm

The Story of Ray & Casey
The Villages, Florida

It was six months before Ray was scheduled to move to his new home in The Villages, a popular retirement community near Orlando, Florida. His canine companion of sixteen years passed away just as he was preparing to make the milestone move. Ray had always had dogs growing up, so it was no wonder that he found himself longing for the patter of paws around the house, once he got settled in.

Casey patiently waiting for Ray to finish swimming in the pool.

About three weeks later, he came across a picture in the paper of Casey, an eight-month-old, twenty-one-pound Chihuahua-Rat Terrier mix, presented by the Georgia-based organization D.A.R.E. Animal Rescue. One of D.A.R.E.'s focuses is to save animals from situations where they're about to be euthanized and foster them until a permanent home can be found, as was the case with Casey.

"Her time was up in the first kennel, and then they moved her to a different place," explains Ray. Casey was very skittish and mistrusting of people. She would get scared and growl and back away from them, making potential adopters feel like she was not a friendly dog. But Casey had a lovely brindle coat, four white paws, and beautiful markings—a unique look that Ray believes bought her some time at each of the shelters. As Casey's time wore thin again, a woman from D.A.R.E. took her in for three weeks and came to find that the dog was actually very affectionate; she just needed the right home.

Casey loves to be taken for a spin around the block in Ray's golf cart.

After Ray inquired about Casey, a couple of D.A.R.E. staff members drove down from Georgia to interview him. The match would have to be just right. Two or three weeks later, they came back with Casey to see how the first meeting would go. Ray was waiting on the lawn when they pulled up.

Casey, the skittish and fearful puppy, ran right up to Ray, as if they'd been separated in a past life. Now, almost two years later, she remains by his side constantly, no matter what he might be doing.

"Wherever I go, she's got to be wherever that is," he says. He could be gone for twenty minutes, but when he returns, Casey acts like it's been forever. She loves to sit at the pool and watch Ray swim. Whenever he exercises, she brings all of her toys to keep him company while he works out.

As Ray was teaching Casey to become housebroken, she quickly fell in love with the outdoors. When she wants to go out—which is frequently—she will ring the Christmas bell Ray hung on the door, sometimes ten or fifteen times a day. Fortunately for both of them, the Florida weather usually cooperates!

"She's bug-crazy," says Ray, "She loves to stay out there and get bugs." Casey will jump in the bushes just to stir up unsuspecting insects, particularly ones that fly, he says. To her dismay, she never actually captures any, but her terrier instincts keep the intrigue of the pursuit fresh.

When Casey isn't stalking bugs, she's patiently waiting in the garage for Ray to take her for a spin on his golf cart. Sometimes, he'll have to drive her around the block, even if he doesn't have anywhere to go, just to get her to come back inside afterward. On Casey's favorite days, they drive it to the dog park.

"She's just changed immensely," says Ray. She's no longer aggressive, all the neighbors know her, and she's very good when company comes to visit. "I get a lot of compliments on her," he says.

Casey is always by Ray's side.

Simply put, he and Casey are inseparable, and that's the way they'd like to keep it.

"I've had all kinds of animals, but a dog is special," concludes Ray, "You can almost hear what they're thinking."

WINE NOT?

Just because Lulu doesn't imbibe, doesn't mean she can't join you for Sunday Funday at a nearby winery. Check online for dog-friendly vineyards in your area and call ahead to make sure you know all the rules and what to expect. To be fully prepared for the day, it's best to pack a leash, water dish, dog food, a couple toys, and bags to clean up after your dog.

Unexpected Discovery

The Story of Simone & Taj
South Deerfield, Massachusetts

It was a hot day in July of 2014 when Simone and her elderly pit bull mix, Bam, headed to their local park in the Bensonhurst section of Brooklyn. They noticed a man on the corner with a black dog, and walked up to say hello. But this wouldn't be their typical morning walk.

The dog didn't belong to the man—he was trying to give him away to anyone who would take him. Simone didn't understand why or what the man was trying to say, but she agreed to take the dog.

Taj is full of energy and loves playing outside.

"I was doing some rescue work in New York City at the time and figured I would have a better chance at finding his owner or a new home," she explains. "The dog was an un-neutered black Lab-pit mix, whose chances of making it out of the shelter alive would have been nearly zero. I knew I had to take him. He was very, very hyper. He was jumping on me and biting the leash in my hand all the way back to the apartment."

Simone discovered several weeks later that the two-year-old pup she had named Tajirius used to belong to a man in the neighborhood who had since gone to prison. He had abandoned Taj, and when the building was sold and the policy was changed to forbid animals, his roommate brought him to the park.

THE GIVING SPIRIT

What better way to celebrate the adoption of your rescue dog than by putting the "fun" in fundraiser at one of your local shelters or Humane Societies? Many organizations host an annual Bark in the Park, Fashion for Paws, or another participatory event for people and their pooches. It's a great way for both of you to socialize while contributing to a worthwhile cause.

Taj and Simone venture out every day, no matter the weather.

"We decided to keep him, even though he was crazy and chased our kittens and ate cords and shoes if left alone for too long," Simone recalls, "He also had bad separation anxiety."

"I call Taj my 'project pup,' but he also helped me find my career path," she explains. "I have been working hard with him and learning more about dog behavior and training. I realized that I wanted to pursue working with animals in some capacity." In the months to follow, Simone moved back to Massachusetts and started working as a dog-walker. Five days a week, in all weather conditions, she takes up to six dogs on long, off-leash hikes through the mountains.

"It's been so much fun—and sometimes stressful—like the time one dog ate an entire deer leg, or when another ran up a tree. I've learned so much about dog behavior and how to manage unruly or difficult dogs. Seeing a dog turn a corner with their training and behavior is the best part of the job," she says. Simone's long-term goal is to start a non-profit rescue with an educational program for kids.

"Rescue dogs are the best pets, because, in some sense, they know that you saved them, and it can be a very special bond," she explains, "It does take patience, especially when the dog is new to your family, but it's worth it a thousand times over when I look at Taj's sweet face and get so much love back from him."

Taj has calmed down quite a bit, though he and Simone still work on clicker training and positive reinforcement, as well as agility training. Taj jumps through hula hoops on command and prances through ladder rungs on the ground in pursuit of a tasty morsel.

Simone does whatever it takes to train Taj, including using non-traditional treats. "He prefers salami and prosciutto over bologna and hot dogs," she chuckles, "Once you find what works for your dog, you can make amazing progress with their training." Taj also loves to play in the wilderness on his twice-daily walks, discovering new hiking trails and running through open fields.

Taj enjoying a wilderness hike.

"He bounds like a happy, fat, little deer through the tall grass," says Simone, "He also likes to wade in streams to catch and eat bubbles, but he doesn't know how to swim yet. I'm trying to figure out how to teach him, but his Lab ancestry is not helping him out much."

When it's indoor time, Taj loves getting new stuffed animals from Goodwill. His newest addition is a stuffed Barney the Dinosaur that he'll proudly show off to you.

"Sometimes I have him wait in another room while I hide a toy, then I'll tell him to find it. This is a fun, easy activity for mental stimulation," says Simone. Much to Barney's chagrin, the toys usually only make it a few weeks … or minutes. "Eventually, he eviscerates them all," she concedes.

At the end of a busy day, it's not unusual for Taj and Simone to be all tuckered out. "I've definitely fallen asleep with him on his dog bed!" she admits. Fortunately, in sleep, there's not much a dog can destroy. Simone will be the first to tell you, "A tired dog is a happy dog!"

RESOURCES

Looking to take a deeper dive on some of the topics covered?
Refer to the below list to get you started on your research.

Books for New Adopters

McConnell, Patricia B. *How to Be the Leader of the Pack … and Have Your Dog Love You for It!*
Wisconsin: McConnell Publishing, 1996.

McConnell, Patricia B. *The Other End of the Leash: Why We Do What We Do Around Dogs.*
New York: Ballentine, 2003.

McKinney, Barbara. *Adopting a Dog: The Indispensable Guide for Your Newest Family Member.*
New York: W. W. Norton & Company, 2005.

Miller, Pat. *Do Over Dogs: Give Your Dog a Second Chance for a First Class Life.*
Wenatchee, WA: Dogwise Publishing, 2010.

Saunders, Kim. *The Adopted Dog Bible: Your One-Stop Resource for Choosing, Training, and Caring for Your Sheltered or Rescued Dog.* New York: William Morrow, 2009.

Sternberg, Sue. *Successful Dog Adoption.* Sternberg, Sue. Hoboken: Howell Book House, 2003.

Online Resources for Dog Behavior and Training

Canine Good Citizen Certificate Information:
http://www.akc.org/dog-owners/training/canine-good-citizen/
Urine Marking in Dogs:
http://www.humanesociety.org/animals/dogs/tips/
urine_marking.html
How to Stop Unwanted Chewing:
http://www.humanesociety.org/animals/dogs/tips/
destructive_chewing.html
Mitigating Fears of Loud Noises:
http://www.humanesociety.org/animals/dogs/tips/fear_thunder_
loud_noises.html
Housetraining Tips:
https://www.petfinder.com/dogs/dog-training/dog-housetraining/
Crate Training Benefits:
https://www.petfinder.com/dogs/dog-training/benefits-dog-crate-training/
Aggression in Dogs:
https://www.aspca.org/pet-care/virtual-pet-behaviorist/dog-behavior/aggression-dogs
Dog Walking Tips:
https://www.aspca.org/pet-care/dog-care/dog-walking-101
Well-Behaved Walking:
https://www.aspca.org/pet-care/virtual-pet-behaviorist/dog-behavior/
teaching-your-dog-not-pull-leash
New Adoption Tips:
http://www.reachoutrescue.org/info/display?PageID=9829

General Tips from The Humane Society of the United States:
http://www.humanesociety.org/animals/dogs/tips/

Online Resources for Dog Care

Grooming Tips from the ASPCA:
https://www.aspca.org/pet-care/dog-care/dog-grooming-tips
Grooming Tips from the Animal Humane Society:
http://www.animalhumanesociety.org/training/grooming-tips-dogs
Bathing:
http://www.aspca.org/pet-care/virtual-pet-behaviorist/dog-behavior/bathing-your-dog
Foods to Avoid:
http://www.aspca.org/pet-care/animal-poison-control/people-foods-avoid-feeding-your-pets
Safety Guidelines for Costumes:
https://www.care.com/a/halloween-pet-costumes-safety-guidelines-1309201614
Beach Safety:
http://www.vets-now.com/pet-owners/dog-care-advice/beach-safety-for-dogs/
Teeth Brushing:
https://www.aspca.org/pet-care/virtual-pet-behaviorist/dog-behavior/brushing-your-dogs-teeth

Nail Trimming:
https://www.aspca.org/pet-care/virtual-pet-behaviorist/dog-behavior/trimming-your-dogs-nails

Nutrition:

https://www.petfinder.com/dogs/dog-nutrition/

How to Read a Dog Food Label:

http://pets.webmd.com/dogs/guide/how-to-read-a-dog-food-label

Emergency Care and First Aid:

http://pets.webmd.com/dogs/guide/dig-emergency-care-first-aid

Recommended Dog Supplies:

http://www.vetstreet.com/our-pet-experts/new-dog-owner-guide-21-items-to-put-on-your-shopping-list

Online Resources for Dog Services

Find Dog Sitters and Dog Walkers Near You:

https://www.rover.com/

https://dogvacay.com/

https://www.sittercity.com/rover?location=20001

National Association of Professional Pet Sitters: http://www.petsitters.org/

Pet Sitters International: https://www.petsit.com/locate

Tips on Selecting a Groomer:

http://www.humanesociety.org/animals/resources/tips/choosing_a_groomer.html

Find a Veterinarian Near You:

http://www.veterinarians.com

ABOUT THE AUTHOR

Alexandra is a devoted animal enthusiast and an
avid supporter of animal shelters and rescues.
She has had the privilege of spending the early part of her career
writing and editing publications for national non-profit organizations
The Humane Society of the United States and the Animal Welfare Institute.
Alexandra lives in Washington, D.C.

Join our online community by sharing your experiences on
Instagram, Facebook, or Twitter with the hashtag **#RescueDogBucketList**

"The great pleasure of a dog
is that you may make a fool of
yourself with him and not only
will he not scold you, but he will
make a fool of himself too."

SAMUEL BUTLER

About Cider Mill Press Book Publishers

Good ideas ripen with time. From seed to harvest,
Cider Mill Press brings fine reading, information,
and entertainment together between the covers of its creatively
crafted books. Our Cider Mill bears fruit twice a year,
publishing a new crop of titles each spring and fall.

Visit us on the Web at
www.cidermillpress.com
or write to us at
12 Spring Street
PO Box 454
Kennebunkport, Maine 04046